DON'T
KNOW
MUCH
ABOUT®

AMERICAN
★★★★★★★★★★★★★★★★★
HISTORY

KENNETH C. DAVIS
ILLUSTRATED BY MATT FAULKNER

📖 HarperCollins*Publishers*

We gratefully acknowledge the sources of the quotes on the following pages: pages 124–125, Thames Television interviews, as reproduced in *Destination America* by Maldwyn A. Jones, copyright © 1976 by Thames Television, published in the United States by Holt, Rinehart & Winston; page 153, reprinted from *Dust Bowl Diary* by Ann Marie Low by permission of the University of Nebraska Press, copyright © 1984 by the University of Nebraska Press.

This is a Don't Know Much About® book.
Don't Know Much About® is the registered trademark of Kenneth C. Davis.

Library of Congress Cataloging-in-Publication Data
Davis, Kenneth C.
  Don't know much about American history / Kenneth C. Davis ; illustrated by Matt Faulkner.—1st ed.
      p.   cm. — (Don't know much about)
  Summary: Presents, in question and answer format, a history of the United States from the exploration of Christopher Columbus to the terrorist attacks of September 11, 2001.
  ISBN 0-06-028603-2 (hardcover) — ISBN 0-06-440836-1 (pbk.)
  ISBN 0-06-028604-0 (lib. bdg.)
  1. United States—History—Juvenile literature.   [1. United States—History—Miscellanea.   2. Questions and answers.]   I. Faulkner, Matt, ill.   II. Title.
E178.3 .D2525   2003   2002151783
973—dc21   CIP
                                                                                        AC

Design by Charles Yuen

1 2 3 4 5 6 7 8 9 10

❖

First Edition

★ ★ ACKNOWLEDGMENTS ★ ★

An author's name goes on the cover of a book. But behind that book are a great many people who make it all happen. I would like to thank all the wonderful people at HarperCollins who helped make this book a reality, including Susan Katz, Kate Morgan Jackson, Barbara Lalicki, Harriett Barton, Rosemary Brosnan, Amy Burton, Meredith Charpentier, Dana Hayward, Maggie Herold, Jeanne Hogle, Rachel Orr, Lorelei Russ, and Sarah Thomson. I would also like to thank David Black, Joy Tutela, and Alix Reid for their friendship, assistance, and great ideas. My wife, Joann, and my children, Jenny and Colin, are always a source of inspiration, joy, and support, and without them my work would not be possible.

I especially thank Kevin P. Kelly, historian at Colonial Williamsburg Foundation, for reviewing the manuscript and providing helpful insights; Matt Faulkner for his clever illustrations; and April Prince for her unique contribution. This book would not have been possible without her tireless work, imagination, and creativity.

T 5519

★★★★ | CONTENTS | ★★★★

When I was nine years old, my folks took me to the famous battlefield at Gettysburg, Pennsylvania. It was the place where, one hundred years earlier, thousands of Americans died fighting one another in the bloodiest three days of the long Civil War. Standing among the rocks at Little Round Top, where young soldiers took cover from bullets and cannonballs, I knew that something special had happened in this place, even if I didn't really understand the Civil War.

View of Little Round Top from Devil's Den

Like most kids back in those days, my friends and I liked to play war games or cowboys and Indians. But that day I understood that this field at Gettysburg was about something real. This was not about make-believe war, but about real people in real places who did real things.

Looking toward Cemetery Hill from Little Round Top

Over the years, as I have spoken to people around the country on talk radio and in bookstores, lecture halls, and classrooms, the one word I usually hear when it comes to history is *"boring!"* To me, history is anything but boring. The stories of what life was actually like for the people who sailed on the *Mayflower* and the Indians they met, or the true stories of pioneers who headed west—these stories are a vital part of what made America the nation it is today.

This book asks a lot of questions about more than five hundred years of history. The answers lie in the remarkable true stories of the men and women, boys and girls who created a country. Sometimes funny, and sometimes sad, I hope you agree that the stories of American history are never boring.

CHAPTER 1

Brave New World

E Pluribus Unum ("Out of Many, One")

—Motto for the Great Seal of the United States

SETTING IT STRAIGHT

Who discovered America?

a) Christopher Columbus

b) Leif Eriksson

c) Amerigo Vespucci

d) the Pilgrims

e) none of the above

The answer is letter *e*. It's true that all the people above came to the Americas. But these Europeans didn't discover what they came to call the "New World" any more than bears discovered honey. The land was just new to them because they hadn't known it existed.

Thousands of years before any European set foot in North America, groups of hunter-gatherers followed bison or woolly mammoths over a land bridge from Asia to present-day Alaska. (Today that land is underwater, but America and Asia are still only fifty-two miles apart near the Arctic Circle.) These people might have arrived as many as thirty thousand or forty thousand years ago. They were certainly here fifteen thousand years ago. Their descendants are called Native Americans or American Indians.

Over thousands of years, American Indians spread through North and South America. Each group adapted to its surroundings and climate. In North America, Indians in the East, upper Midwest, and Northwest hunted in the forests and mountains and fished in the lakes, streams, and oceans. Some farmed the land. They lived in wigwams or wood houses. On the plains many Indian tribes hunted the bison that roamed the open prairies. They lived in teepees or thatched grass houses. And in the Southwest some farmed and carved houses and cities into the sides of cliffs. There may have been between 50 million and 100 million Indians and more than two thousand distinct cultures in North and South America.

Was Christopher Columbus the first European in the Americas?

Nope. As far as historians know, that title goes to the Norseman Erik the Red, who beat Columbus by a good five hundred years. Erik the Red sailed west from Scandinavia and came upon Greenland in the year 982. He started a small colony there. Then around the year 1000, his son Leif Eriksson (get it—son of Erik?) sailed even farther west to what is now Canada. Leif and his men spent the winter before returning to Greenland. Other Norse colonists stayed for three years or so but, finding the native people none too friendly, eventually returned as well. The remains of what was probably their settlement—some houses, workshops, and a forge—can be seen today at L'Anse aux Meadows in Newfoundland. Though this was the first known European settlement in the New World, the Norse didn't leave a lasting impression. That was left to an enterprising sailor named Christopher Columbus.

Why don't all Americans celebrate Columbus Day?

Columbus landed in the islands of the Caribbean in 1492, hundreds of years after the Norsemen came to North America

Italian explorer Christopher Columbus

and thousands of years after American Indians reached the continent. So what's Columbus Day all about, aside from getting a day off from school?

Columbus's "discovery" of a land previously unknown to most Europeans changed the world forever. His arrival in the New World marked the beginning of an extraordinary era of European discovery, conquest, and colonization in the Americas. What's been called the "Columbian exchange" brought together people who'd been separated for fifteen thousand years. These people began sharing ideas, foods, crops, animals, languages, cultures, and religions, enriching both the Old and New Worlds.

Yet not everyone thinks this is something to celebrate. What was good for Europeans was devastating to American Indians. Europeans brought deadly diseases to the Americas that the natives couldn't fight off. Within 150 years, an estimated 85 percent of the American population had died—perhaps 64 million to 85 million Indians. Nor did Africans benefit from Columbus's discovery, since many were later taken from their homelands to work as slaves in the New World. So Columbus Day marks a meeting of cultures that had both good and bad effects on the people of the world.

Why isn't America called Columbia?

Because a mapmaker didn't think of him in time. Columbus died thinking he'd reached the East Indies. (That's why he named the native people "Indians.") But explorers who came after him soon realized the land across the Atlantic was entirely new to them. The first person to put this into writing was an Italian businessman named Amerigo Vespucci, who sailed to South America in 1499, 1501, and 1503. In a letter Vespucci claimed to have found a "*Mundus Novus,*" or New

World. The idea of a New World was exciting, and Vespucci's travels became more famous in his day than Columbus's.

When a mapmaker named Martin Waldseemüller created an updated map of the world in 1507, he named South America in honor of Vespucci. Afterward Waldseemüller felt he'd made a mistake in doing so and removed the name from a later map. But it was too late. The name "America" was already being used all over Europe, and it became attached to the North American continent as well.

Who followed Columbus to America?

Several European countries sent sailors on the heels of Columbus. Some of these sailors began to search for a "Northwest Passage," or an all-water route through the Americas to the East. (The only practical Northwest Passage that exists is so far north that its waters are frozen most of the year, but Europeans didn't know that yet.) The search led them into the interior of North and South America, where they realized that the land was not a roadblock to Asia but a major opportunity. There were riches to plunder, land to claim, and natives to convert to Christianity.

The key players in the exploration of the Americas were the Spanish, French, and English; the Portuguese, Dutch, and Swedes had minor roles.

• The Spanish explored, claimed land, or started settlements in present-day California, Arizona, New Mexico, Texas, Florida, Mexico, and much of South and Central America in the 1500s.

• The Portuguese began to settle Brazil in 1532.

• The English made a claim in the 1580s. Within seventy-five years, thirteen British colonies would line the east coast of what would become the United States.

• The French laid claim to Canada with the explorations of Jacques Cartier in the 1530s. Father Jacques Marquette and Louis Joliet traveled down the Mississippi River in 1673, stretching French holdings in North America from Canada and the Great Lakes to the Gulf of Mexico. (This territory was named Louisiana, after the French king Louis XIV.)

• The Dutch established New Amsterdam on the Hudson River in 1625. Before long the Dutch took over a small colony of Swedes, who had settled in what is now Delaware in 1638. New Amsterdam was, in turn, captured by the English in 1664 and became New York.

⭐ Because of the gold and silver they found in central Mexico, the Spaniards believed many legends about the riches of the New World. Explorers went looking for the famed city of El Dorado (Spanish for "the golden one"), the Seven Cities of Cíbola, and the magical Fountain of Youth. None of these was ever found (because they don't exist), though the thirst for riches was so great that many Europeans died trying. Still, the Spaniards' searches led them to travel across—and lay claim to— about one third of the land that would eventually become the southwestern United States.

LAND HO! EUROPEANS COME TO NORTH AMERICA, 1492–1620

1492   Sailing for the Spanish crown, Italian navigator Christopher Columbus crosses the ocean blue (and lands in the Bahamas).

1497   Italian navigator Giovanni Caboto (John Cabot), sailing for England, lands in Newfoundland and claims it for England.

1513   Juan Ponce de León, the first European to set foot in what is now the United States, lands in Florida.

1534   Jacques Cartier sails up the St. Lawrence River and claims the territory for France.

1540   Spain's Francisco de Coronado explores New Mexico and the American Southwest.

1565   Spaniards settle St. Augustine, Florida.

1585   The English establish a colony in Roanoke, Virginia (present-day North Carolina).

1607   The first permanent English settlement in the New World is founded in Jamestown, Virginia.

1608   French explorer Samuel de Champlain founds Quebec, Canada.

1609   Henry Hudson, sailing for the Dutch, explores what is now New York's Hudson River.

1614   After leaving the Jamestown settlement, John Smith explores the New England coast.

1620   The Pilgrims settle at Plymouth, Massachusetts.

If the Spanish got here first, why don't Americans speak Spanish?

Americans don't speak Spanish because the Spanish didn't control the northern colonies that became the first states. The Spanish had the most influence in South and Central America, as well as in the lands that are now Florida, Texas, New Mexico, Arizona, and California. The French, English, and Dutch settled in the northeast, with the English gradually taking control. When the United States became independent, it was made up of former English colonies. Yet history is continuously being written. During your lifetime, people of Hispanic heritage will probably replace blacks as the largest ethnic group in the United States—which means more and more Americans will be speaking Spanish as well as English.

What do a river in New York and a bay in Canada have in common?

Their name. Both the Hudson River and Hudson Bay were named after English explorer Henry Hudson. While searching for the Northwest Passage to Asia in 1609, Hudson sailed up and down the east coast of North America, including a brief trip part of the way up the river now called the Hudson. He didn't find the Northwest Passage on that trip, and two years later in 1611 he had even worse luck. Looking for the passage farther north in Canada, Hudson and his crew became trapped in ice. The starving crew mutinied and forced Hudson, his son, and six crew members into a small boat, which was cast adrift. The castaways were never heard from again.

 ## The Pilgrims established the first successful English settlement in North America.

False. In 1607, thirteen years before the Pilgrims arrived at Plymouth, a group of Englishmen sailed to Virginia. They hoped to find gold, silver, and copper that would make them—and the owners of the Virginia Company of London, which funded their trip—rich. The 105 men (there were no women or children at first) landed at a place they named Jamestown, after England's King James.

Like the settlers at Roanoke, the Jamestown colonists struggled for survival. Within a few months of their landing, about half the colonists had died. There was little to eat because the sea voyage had taken longer than they expected, and the rations that remained were full of worms. Few of the first colonists knew how to farm or were very interested in working. Most of the colonists were English gentlemen unaccustomed to hard labor, and many preferred to search for gold. On top of all that, Jamestown could hardly have been in a worse location. The land was swampy, the drinking water bad, and the climate extremely hot in summer and cold in winter.

The colony stumbled along for several years, as new settlers, including women and children, arrived. Jamestown ultimately survived, partly because of the strict leadership of a short, red-bearded man named Captain John Smith; partly because of the food the local Indians provided; and mostly because of the tobacco plant. The settlers never found gold, but they did grow tobacco, which they discovered was just as valuable. They sold it to England by the ton, even though King James said smoking was "a custom loathsome to the eye, hateful to the nose, harmful to the brain, dangerous to the lungs."

Did Pocahontas save John Smith's life?

Pocahontas saves Smith from the Algonquins.

As the third leader of Jamestown, John Smith was not always popular. But he was fair, hardworking, and brave, and he did more than anyone else to make sure the struggling colony survived. His policy was "He who does not work, will not eat." He traded with the Indians for food and learned their language and hunting and fishing methods. Yet relations with the Indians remained unpredictable, so he also strengthened defenses against them.

In one famous story, Smith was captured and brought before the great Chief Powhatan. During a ceremony, in which Captain Smith was unsure of his fate, the young Indian princess Pocahontas laid her head across Smith's and pleaded with her father, Powhatan, to let the Englishman live. Smith wrote down this story years later, which made many people think he made it up or embellished it. (He was known to be a boastful man.) Pocahontas's act may have been a customary or planned part of the ceremony. Either way, the Indians made Smith an honorary chief of their tribe.

The life of the real Pocahontas was quite different from the story you might have seen in the movies. She was only twelve when the settlers first arrived. Years later, after Smith left Jamestown, Pocahontas met and married an English settler named John Rolfe. Traveling with him to England, she adopted English clothing and became well known in her adopted land as Rebecca. Sadly, she eventually fell sick with smallpox, dying at age twenty-two.

Who lived at the House of Burgesses?

No one, because the House wasn't a place but a group of lawmakers. The House of Burgesses, patterned after British local government (whose representatives were called burgesses), was a group of lawmakers made up of Jamestown colonists. The Virginia Company of London created the group in 1619 to give the colonists a say in their own government. Instead of obeying laws made by appointed colonial governors or by the British Parliament in faraway England, the colonists would make their own laws. The House of Burgesses wasn't the first representative government in America—some Indian tribes had them—but it was a first step toward self-government for English colonists.

Did all people come to the New World to get rich?

No, though many came in hopes of making a better life. Some came to start religious communities. Some came for land. Others came as *indentured servants*, who hired themselves out to work for someone else for four to seven years to pay for their voyage. Many who came as servants were poor, unskilled laborers who wanted to escape poverty and crowding in Europe. Most were young, single men about sixteen to twenty-seven years of age, but women and children crossed the ocean as servants, too. Servants had almost no legal rights and could be treated as badly as slaves—it all depended on the master.

Still others came to America against their will: Black Africans were first brought to Jamestown in 1619. Though these black immigrants were listed as servants, it wasn't long before they were treated as slaves. Europeans soon realized that Africans would make better slaves than Indians would. They didn't catch as many European diseases, and there were plenty of them with nowhere to run to, unlike the local Indians. An awful institution—slavery—had begun in what would later become the United States.

Almost every European nation and African empire made huge profits from the slave trade. Slavery was common in Africa before Europeans arrived, but when the European slave trade began, African rulers began raiding other villages specifically to capture slaves to sell to European traders. Africans of any rank might be ripped from their homelands and families and marched to the coast to be sold and loaded onto overcrowded ships. There they were chained together belowdecks and forced to sit or lie in their own waste with barely enough room to move. The dehumanizing journey to America could take from five weeks to three months. Historians estimate that one in six Africans died along the way.

Between about 1500 and 1800, about 12 million African slaves were brought to the New World in a system called the "triangular trade." On the first leg of this triangle, ships filled with trade goods such as textiles and guns left England and landed on the West African coast. Africans who had been kidnapped were exchanged for these goods and taken on the second leg of the journey, the "Middle Passage" to the Americas. There slave traders sold them for sugar, tobacco, cotton, grain, and rice, and the ships headed back to England. About 5 million slaves went to the Caribbean and more than 6 million to Central and South America. Only about a half million came to the English colonies that would become the United States.

AMERICAN VOICES

66 ONE DAY, WHEN ALL OUR PEOPLE WERE GONE OUT TO THEIR WORKS AS USUAL, AND ONLY I AND MY DEAR SISTER WERE LEFT TO MIND THE HOUSE, TWO MEN AND A WOMAN GOT OVER OUR WALLS, AND IN A MOMENT SEIZED US BOTH, AND, WITHOUT GIVING US TIME TO CRY OUT, OR MAKE RESISTANCE, THEY STOPPED OUR MOUTHS, AND RAN OFF WITH US INTO THE NEAREST WOOD. HERE THEY TIED OUR HANDS. . . . MY CRIES HAD NO OTHER EFFECT THAN TO MAKE THEM TIE ME FASTER AND STOP MY MOUTH, AND THEN THEY PUT ME INTO A LARGE SACK. . . . THE NEXT DAY

PROVED A DAY OF GREATER SORROW THAN I HAD YET EXPERIENCED; FOR MY SISTER AND I WERE THEN SEPARATED, WHILE WE LAY CLASPED IN EACH OTHER'S ARMS. IT WAS IN VAIN THAT WE BESOUGHT THEM NOT TO PART US; SHE WAS TORN FROM ME, AND IMMEDIATELY CARRIED AWAY. . . .**"**

—OLAUDAH EQUIANO, *an African born to a noble family, taken into slavery when he was just a boy*

After eleven years as a slave, Equiano was freed. He published his autobiography in 1789, in hopes that his description of the evils of slavery would help end the dreadful institution.

Who were the Pilgrims?

The *Mayflower* arrives in Plymouth Harbor.

The Pilgrims were part of a religious group of English men and women called *Puritans*. Puritans disagreed with some of the ideas of the Church of England, especially its elaborate ceremonies and decorations. They wanted to purify the Church. The Pilgrims were a group of Puritans who didn't just want to purify the Church, they wanted to break away from it altogether. But in the Puritans' day, all English people had to belong to the Church of England and none other. So King James told the Pilgrims to shape up or ship out. You know what they chose.

The name "Pilgrim" comes from a book one of the Pilgrims, William Bradford, wrote many years after the *Mayflower*—the ship that brought the settlers to the New World—landed. He called his fellow settlers "pilgrims" because a pilgrim is someone who takes a pilgrimage, or a long journey to a holy land. Fewer than half of the 102 passengers on board the

Mayflower were Puritans. The others were Englishmen seeking adventure or a better life in America. Yet even though not everyone aboard the *Mayflower* was a religious pilgrim, William Bradford's word seemed to capture the spirit of the new settlers best, and the whole group of settlers has become known as Pilgrims.

 An Indian walked into Plymouth and said, "Welcome, Englishmen."

True! The Indian was an Algonquian chief named Samoset, from what is now Maine. Samoset had traveled to Plymouth with an English explorer and had learned to speak English from British fishermen. He introduced the Pilgrims to his friend Tisquantum, or Squanto, who also spoke English. Squanto was the Pilgrims' greatest friend. He showed them how to hunt and catch fish, which herbs were safe to eat, and how to grow corn. Many Pilgrims died the first winter, but all of them might have perished if it hadn't been for Squanto's help.

Squanto lived with the Pilgrims for the rest of his life. He helped them negotiate a peace treaty with Chief Massasoit of the Wampanoag Indians. It was these Indians with whom the Pilgrims celebrated their first harvest in October 1621. The Pilgrims and Indians spent three days playing games and feasting on wild turkey, duck, deer, seafood, corn, carrots, cabbages, turnips, beets, onions, and cornmeal pies. The Pilgrims didn't have pumpkin pie or cranberry sauce, but they did have pumpkins and cranberries.

The first national Thanksgiving was proclaimed by George Washington in 1789. The country celebrated the holiday off and on—mostly off—until 1863, when President Abraham Lincoln established it as a yearly national holiday. In 1941 Congress set the date of the fourth Thursday in November, the day on which Americans celebrate today.

AMERICAN ★ STORIES

Roger Williams was a Puritan minister, but he didn't share the strict attitudes of some of his fellow ministers. In fact, he said that "forced worship stinks in God's nostrils."

Williams helped settle the Massachusetts Bay Colony, which Puritans—inspired by the Pilgrims' success—started in Boston in 1631. He soon found that his strict, idealistic fellow Puritans wanted religious freedom, but only for themselves. They were quick to whip, jail, banish, or even hang non-Puritans. Williams, charming and well liked in person, angered other ministers when he wrote books criticizing this intolerance. Unsure what to do with him at first, the Puritans decided to put Williams on a boat back to England. Before they could do that, Roger Williams ran away and founded the city of Providence, Rhode Island. In Rhode Island Williams said each person could choose his or her own religion. And because Roger Williams believed in the separation of church and state ("state" meaning government), men of any religion could vote. Though other colonies would practice religious toleration, Rhode Island was the only one founded for this purpose.

Did the Dutch really buy all of Manhattan Island for $24?

Yes and no. They actually bought it with beads, cloth, and hatchets.

Manhattan Island is the main part of present-day New York City. But before Manhattan was the nation's bustling center of banking, book publishing, art, and fashion, it was part of the Dutch city of New Amsterdam. In one of the most famous real-estate deals in American history, Peter Minuit, the leader of New Amsterdam, bought all of Manhattan Island from the local Indians for about 60 Dutch guilders' worth of beads, cloth, and hatchets. That 1626 sum was converted about 250 years later to 2,400 English cents, or $24. (Today $24 will buy you a parking space in Manhattan for about an hour!)

New Netherland, the colony that included New Amsterdam, grew as the Dutch settled on surrounding land. In 1664 the British took over all of New Netherland and renamed it New York, in honor of the Duke of York, Britain's future king.

All colonial leaders bought their land from the Indians.

Sadly, the answer is false; many just took the land without paying. However, a few leaders did buy their land. The Dutch purchased Manhattan, and Roger Williams bought land to start Providence. Another man who believed in religious freedom, William Penn, paid the Indians for land that is now part of Pennsylvania.

William Penn was among the few Europeans to treat Indians as equals. Penn was a member of a religious group called the Society of Friends, commonly known as Quakers. Quakers believe that everyone is equal and has inner light that leads him or her to God. (The strength of their feeling sometimes caused people to shake, or quake, hence the term "Quaker.") Quakers don't believe in swearing allegiance to any authority but God—a view that was threatening to people in power. Quakers had been imprisoned in England and chased out of every colony but Rhode Island.

William Penn founded Pennsylvania, meaning "Penn's woods."

William Penn's Pennsylvania was founded as a colony for Quakers, but it was open to everyone. (The name of its major city, Philadelphia, comes from two Greek words that mean "brotherly love.") The Quakers were among the first colonists to oppose slavery, and later in American history they would be at the forefront of other nonviolent movements for justice and equal rights.

Can you name the thirteen original British colonies?

It's not as easy as you might think! Most, but not all, of the states that run along the east coast of the United States today were among the thirteen original colonies. (Some hints to get you started: Don't include Maine, which was part of Massachusetts, nor Florida, which belonged to Spain.) Turn the page to check your answers.

COLONY	YEAR FOUNDED	FOUNDERS
Virginia	1607	Settlers of the Virginia Company of London
Massachusetts	1620	Pilgrims and Puritans, for their own religious freedom
New Hampshire	1623	English colonists who had a land grant from Britain
New York	1626	Dutch, for trading purposes; the British took over in 1664
Maryland	1632	Lord Baltimore, as a safe place for Catholics
Rhode Island	1636	Roger Williams, who was banished from Massachusetts for religious reasons
Connecticut	1636	Thomas Hooker, who led a group from Massachusetts
Delaware	1638	Swedish, then Dutch; the British were given the land in 1664
North Carolina	1653	Settlers from Virginia, many of whom wanted more religious freedom
South Carolina	1663	British, and French for religious freedom
New Jersey	1664	Dutch and Swedish; Englishmen were granted land by the Duke of York
Pennsylvania	1682	William Penn, as a haven for Quakers
Georgia	1732	James Oglethorpe, who brought debtors released from English prisons to give them a new life, and built a *Utopian*, or ideal, society

Life in Connecticut was just like life in South Carolina.

False. Colonists, like the Indians before them, had to make do with the climate and resources available where they settled. These factors, combined with the settlers' backgrounds and religions, shaped regional ways of life in New England (Connecticut, Massachusetts, New Hampshire, Rhode Island), the Middle Colonies (Delaware, New Jersey, New York, Pennsylvania), and the Southern Colonies (Georgia, Maryland, North Carolina, South Carolina, Virginia):

• In New England most people lived in towns or on small farms nearby. Towns were often founded by groups of people who knew one another in England, many of whom were members of the Congregational Church. (Congregationalism grew out of the Puritan movement.) Boys often went to school for a few weeks in the winter, when they weren't needed on the farm, while girls were usually taught by their parents at home. If your father wasn't a farmer, he might be a fisherman, a lumberman, or a shipbuilder.

• The Middle Colonies had more diverse populations. Even though the colonies were British, not all the colonists were. Much of the area had been settled by the Dutch and Swedish before the British took over, and were joined by German and Scottish immigrants. In the Middle Colonies many people were Quakers. Each church had a school that was funded by the government, and most children attended. The economy of the Middle Colonies combined farming and the manufacture of glass, leather goods, barrels, guns, and tools.

• The Southern Colonies were settled by a mix of British immigrants and other Europeans who practiced several religions, mostly Protestant. In the South the land and climate were especially good for farming. Most families lived on small farms that produced tobacco, rice, or indigo (a plant grown for its blue dye), but some lived on large plantations where slaves did most of the work. Since families generally lived far apart from one another, there were few schools in the Southern Colonies. Wealthy parents often hired teachers or sent their children to school in England.

AMERICAN VOICES

❝Fix'd gown for Prude,—Mend Mother's Riding-hood,—Spun short thread,—Fix'd two gowns for Welsh's girls,—Carded tow,—Spun linen,—Worked on Cheese-basket,—Hatchel'd flax with Hannah, we did 51 lbs. Apiece,—Pleasted and ironed,—Read a Sermon of Dodridge's—Spooled a piece,—Milked the cows,—Spun linen, did 50 knots,—Made a Broom of Guinea wheat straw,—Spun

THREAD TO WHITEN,—SET A RED DYE,—HAD TWO SCHOLARS
FROM MRS. TAYLOR'S,—I CARDED TWO POUNDS OF WHOLE WOOL
AND FELT NATIONLY,—SPUN HARNESS TWINE,—SCOURED THE
PEWTER. **99**

— ABIGAIL FOOTE, *a young Connecticut girl who listed these chores in
her diary in 1775*

GREAT AMERICAN PASTIMES

Which of the following might you have played as a colonial kid?

a) basketball
b) hopscotch

c) Frisbee
d) miniature golf

The answer is letter *b*. There wasn't much time to play in colonial days, but kids squeezed in games of tag, blindman's bluff, London bridge, hopscotch (then called scotch hopping), or hide-and-seek. If you were very lucky, you might have a spinning top, cornhusk or rag doll, or a set of checkers (called checks), dominoes, jacks, marbles, or cards. Favorite summertime activities included kite flying, berry picking, swimming, and fishing. In the winter there were sledding and ice skating.

In quieter times you might read a book. There were no books written especially for kids' entertainment, so children read their parents' *Robinson Crusoe*, *Gulliver's Travels*, and *Aesop's Fables*. The most popular title in the colonies is still America's top seller today. Can you guess what it is? (The answer is below.)

Answer: The Bible

CHAPTER 2

A Little Rebellion

"The distinctions between Virginians, Pennsylvanians, New Yorkers, New Englanders are no more. I am not a Virginian but an American."

—PATRICK HENRY, *speech in the First Continental Congress, 1774*

What did the Indians think of the colonists?

At first the Indians greeted the colonists in peace. Many settlers owed their lives to the Indians and the valuable knowledge they shared on hunting, fishing, and planting crops. Some Indians also traded furs and food for guns, metal hatchets, brass kettles, and steel needles. Many tried to live in harmony with the strange newcomers.

★ Even though it's common to think of Indians as scalp-takers, colonists also used the tactic to control the "Indian problem." Some colonies offered rewards for dead Indians or their scalps.

But any peace was a fragile one. As more Europeans came and settled on Indian land, tensions rose. In New England suspicions and accusations erupted into two bloody and costly wars. The first occurred in 1637, when Puritans burned Pequot villages in the Connecticut River valley. The Indians fought back, but were nearly wiped out.

The Pequot War was a taste of what was to come in King Philip's War in Massachusetts nearly forty years later, in 1675. The mood had changed since the Pilgrims and Wampanoags signed their peace treaty in the 1620s. Chief Massasoit's son Metacom, called King Philip by the English for his adoption of European dress and customs, was eager to strike back at the Englishmen who were destroying his land. When he did, the fighting was brutal and bloody. There was scalping on both sides, and King Philip himself was killed.

Why did some colonists live with the Indians?

Almost from the time Indians and Europeans came into contact in America, Indians took colonists as captives. Most were taken during battles or as a kind of payment for Indians killed or sold into slavery by the colonists. Some captives became slaves, but others were adopted into the Indians' tribe. Of these, one of the most famous was a seven-year-old girl named Eunice Williams.

Eunice lived with her family in Deerfield, Massachusetts, a settlement that was raided and burned many times before Eunice, her family, and about a hundred others were captured by Mohawk and Abenaki raiders in 1704. The captives who weren't killed were made to march hundreds of miles to Canada. During the march, Eunice became separated from her family. Her surviving family members were freed two years later, but Eunice wasn't seen again by an Englishman until she was sixteen. By then she had married an Indian man and couldn't be convinced to come home. Though she visited Massachusetts several times, she lived with her adopted tribe until she died at age eighty-nine.

SETTING IT STRAIGHT

Did frontiersman Daniel Boone wear a coonskin cap?

No, though he's often shown that way in pictures, movies, and television shows. But cap or no, Daniel Boone (1734–1820) deserves his fame as a legend of the American frontier. Even during his lifetime, Boone was the very picture of the rugged outdoorsman. He became one of the first and best-known "long hunters," or mountain men, who spent months, sometimes years, in the wilderness hunting deer, beaver, buffalo, and other animals for their skins. Life as a mountain man was dangerous; Boone was captured several times by Indians and either escaped or was released. He was a friend to some Indians and a foe to others, as he saw fit.

One of Boone's most important jobs was opening the Wilderness Road through the narrow Cumberland Gap in the

Appalachian Mountains in 1775. The road would lead settlers from North Carolina to land called Kentucky. Working his way along Indian and bison trails, Boone and thirty other men rolled away rocks, hacked down trees and brush, and put *blazes*, or marks, on trees so settlers would know which way to go. At the end of the three-hundred-mile trail, they settled a town called Boonesborough. By 1800 there were seven hundred thousand settlers west of the Appalachians. They outnumbered the Indians in the area by eight to one.

What's the best pet for a free and democratic society?

A "watchdog," or a free press that informs the public if and when its government officials are up to no good.

The foundations of freedom of the press in America were laid in 1735, when a New York printer named John Peter Zenger was put on trial for libel. (*Libel* is a published statement that unjustly says something bad about a person and thereby causes him or her harm, like loss of a job.) Zenger printed that the royal governor of New York took bribes, stole people's land, and rigged elections. Saying those things was harmful to the governor. But those things were true.

In those days it was against the law to say anything bad about the king of England or his representatives in the colonies. Zenger's lawyer argued that his client could not be convicted because everything he printed was true. The jury agreed and *acquitted* Zenger, or found him not guilty. The decision showed that the jurors didn't feel bound to English civil law, even though the colonists were British citizens. The case also laid the foundation for our democratic freedom of the press by saying that true statements cannot be considered libel. That freedom to speak out was an important weapon in the protests that led up to the American Revolution.

Who fought the French and Indian War?

It wasn't the French against the Indians, but the French and their Indian *allies*, or friends, against the British and their Indian allies. The war was fought because both European countries claimed the same valuable land around North America's Great Lakes and Ohio and Mississippi Rivers. Whoever won the war would dominate the continent.

At the start of the war, there were about 1,500,000 British citizens and about 90,000 French citizens in the colonies. The French, though outnumbered, were better fighters and had most of the Indians on their side. The Indians sided with the French because they were the lesser of two evils. The French mostly wanted to trade and trap beaver, not colonize and take over land. Additionally, French missionaries went to live with the Indians and learned their customs and language, whereas the British generally took over land, mistreated the Indians, and ignored their cultures.

The first shots of the French and Indian War were fired in 1754 when a twenty-one-year-old lieutenant colonel named George Washington was sent to Fort Duquesne in western Pennsylvania to force out the French—they were on British territory. But the French had no intention of leaving, and they promptly defeated the young and inexperienced colonel and his 150 men. Washington returned the following year under British General Edward Braddock, and again the British met defeat. Braddock died; Washington escaped after two horses were shot out from under him and four bullet holes were made in his coat.

The war went in favor of the French until William Pitt took over the British army in 1758. Pitt appointed new commanders, who won a string of victories and eventually the war. The Treaty of Paris, signed in 1763, sent France packing from North America, except for two tiny islands off the coast of Canada. The French territory west of the Mississippi River went to Spain (which had helped France briefly in the war), and everything else—all of Canada, America east of the Mississippi, and some Caribbean islands—went to the British.

AMERICAN PORTRAITS
George Washington

More than six feet tall, powerful, and very strong, George Washington (1732–1799) was serious, but not stern. Washington became famous for his service during the French and Indian War, and in 1775 he was unanimously chosen to command the Continental army. He may not have been the most brilliant general in history, but Washington inspired his poorly trained, poorly clothed, and poorly fed soldiers to victory. One thing we know for sure is that Washington became the first larger-than-life American hero. He retired to his family estate at Mount Vernon, Virginia, after the war, but in 1789 was called to serve as the nation's first president. He was so beloved by his countrymen that some people wanted to crown him king, an idea Washington vehemently rejected. Despite his desire to remain a private citizen, Washington led the fragile new nation for eight years.

How did sugar and stamps help start the American Revolution?

It wasn't the sugar and the stamps themselves, but the taxes placed on them that got the colonists fired up.

After the French and Indian War, Britain had huge debts to pay. The king and the British *Parliament*, or the group of officials chosen to help the king make laws, assumed that the colonists would help pay the debt, since it was racked up partially in their defense. The result was the Sugar Act of 1764, which placed taxes on sugar, coffee, wine, and other items imported to the colonies from Britain. The even stronger Stamp Act, passed in 1765, taxed everything printed on paper, from newspapers to playing cards.

The colonists didn't object to doing their part, but they did object to not being asked about it. They were angry at being told what to do by a mother country three thousand miles away. They were especially angry at being taxed without being represented in Parliament. King George III, who had come to the throne in 1760, was stubborn and vain, though it was really Parliament that held the power in Britain.

A group of colonists called the Sons of Liberty refused to be treated like second-class citizens. These patriots started riots and encouraged the boycotting not just of paper goods but of all British imports. British merchants complained, as they lost money when colonists refused to buy their goods. Britain repealed the Stamp Act in 1766, but the fight was just getting warmed up.

Why was the naming of the Boston Massacre only a half truth?

The event did take place in Boston, so it's the "massacre" that's the falsehood.

What has come down in history as the Boston Massacre was a skirmish prompted by rising tensions between the British and

the colonists. Not having learned a thing from the colonists' anger at the Sugar and Stamp Acts, in 1767 Parliament imposed the Townshend Acts. These taxed lead, tea, paper, paint, and glass imported into the colonies.

Paul Revere's famous engraving of the "massacre" on King Street

Once again the colonists boycotted, refusing to buy these products. But this time British troops were ordered to enforce the laws. There were four thousand Redcoats, or British soldiers, in Boston, a city of only sixteen thousand. In 1770 Redcoats in front of Boston's Customs House were taunted by a mob of angry colonists who began throwing snow, ice, and stones at the soldiers. The Redcoats panicked. One of them heard, or thought he heard, the word "fire"—and fire he did. Other Redcoats joined in, killing five colonists, including a former slave named Crispus Attucks.

A massacre? Hardly. (A *massacre* is when a great number of people are killed in an especially violent or cruel way.) Yet some patriots used the incident to their advantage. Samuel Adams and Paul Revere of Boston published their own versions of the event: Revere's included an engraving of orderly British troops firing into a group of peaceful, unarmed colonials. Copies of the image spread like wildfire, and within days the incident was known as the Boston Massacre. Colonists were outraged. As a result, the Redcoats were removed from the city and the colonies. But the peace was fragile at best.

Benjamin Franklin

In his day, Benjamin Franklin (1706–1790) was the most famous and admired American in the world. The fifteenth of seventeen children, he was largely self-educated and went on to become a great writer, diplomat, printer, scientist, and inventor. He grew rich publishing a newspaper, the *Pennsylvania Gazette*, and his own magazine, *Poor Richard's Almanack*. In addition to forecasting the weather and telling when the moon would be full, the *Almanack* gave advice like "Early to bed and early to rise, makes a man healthy, wealthy and wise," "A penny saved is a penny earned," and "Three may keep a secret, if two of them are dead."

Ben retired from printing at age forty-two to study, invent, and become a statesman. He started America's first public library and volunteer fire department and Pennsylvania's first university and public hospital. When he dared to fly a kite in a thunderstorm, he showed that lightning bolts were just huge electric sparks. He invented the lightning rod, bifocal glasses, the efficient Franklin stove, and many other things. And though he once had great affection for the British, he was so insulted and verbally abused by the king's government while serving as Pennsylvania's agent in London that he returned to America a complete patriot. Franklin would find his way into many historic scenes of the American Revolution. He penned this satirical ballad:

We have an old mother that peevish is grown
She snubs us like children that scarce walk alone
She forgets we're grown up and have sense of our own
Which nobody can deny, deny, which nobody can deny.
If we don't obey orders whatever the case;
She frowns, and she chides and she loses all patience
And sometimes she hits us a slap in the face
Which nobody can deny, deny, which nobody can deny.

How did Boston Harbor become the biggest teapot in history?

It was December 1773, and the rabble-rousing patriot Sam Adams was at it again. He and his wealthy friend John Hancock were hatching a plan to protest the Parliament's tea tax and its unfair policies on the sale of the tea that colonists drank every day. (Parliament granted the British East India Company the right to sell tea directly to the colonies without paying the taxes colonial merchants had to pay. This advantage allowed the company to undersell colonial merchants and effectively cut them out of the profitable tea trade.) When three tea-laden British ships arrived in Boston Harbor, a group of about a hundred Bostonians, including Adams, Hancock, and Paul Revere, refused to let the tea land. They disguised themselves as Mohawk Indians and boarded the ships. Then they spent three hours splitting open 342 chests of expensive tea and dumping them into the water, while a large crowd looked on.

The Boston Tea Party, as it was quickly named, spurred "tea parties" in other colonies. It also created a more visible division between the Patriots (also called Whigs), who supported liberty, and the Loyalists (also called Tories), who were loyal to the British crown. Over in England, the Tea Party made King George and Parliament very angry. As punishment, Parliament passed even stricter laws for rebellious Massachusetts. These Intolerable Acts, as the colonists called them, banned town meetings, required colonists to provide food and shelter to British troops, and closed Boston Harbor until the waterlogged tea was paid for. The closing of the harbor put many Bostonians out of work. Even worse, it threatened starvation by keeping food from entering the city.

Though the Intolerable Acts were aimed at Massachusetts, people in the other twelve colonies realized that Britain would not hesitate to treat any of them just as harshly. The colonies bonded together as never before, each sending food and other goods to help the people of Boston. Patriots and Loyalists alike knew it was only a matter of time before the first shots were fired in the American Revolution. King George knew it, too. "The die is now cast," he said. "The colonies must either submit or triumph."

⭐ As colonists' frustrations with Britain mounted, intercolonial "commitees of correspondence" were established. These committees kept one another informed of events and were the first real contact and support among the colonies. Until this time, the colonies had been much more closely tied to London than to one another.

How did the colonists tolerate the Intolerable Acts?

They didn't. The Intolerable Acts would backfire against Britain even more than the other laws and taxes had. The Intolerable Acts helped the colonists realize they had common problems, and a meeting was called to bring patriots together to discuss their growing concerns. Fifty-five delegates from every colony but Georgia convened in Philadelphia in 1774 as the First Continental Congress. (Georgia had an especially strong royal governor whom the Georgians didn't want to defy, though they did vow to support the actions taken at the meeting.) Among the delegates were George Washington, Patrick Henry, John Adams, Samuel Adams, and eventually Benjamin Franklin—an assembly John Adams noted in his diary was comprised of "a collection of the greatest Men upon this Continent."

The First Continental Congress was an important turning point in the minds of the delegates. The congress passed a declaration of the rights of the colonists (which were merely the rights due all British citizens) and wrote a polite petition to King George asking him to consider their grievances. It also formed a Continental Association in which the members pledged not to import British goods and to stop exporting goods to Britain. The delegates agreed to return the following May if they hadn't made any headway with the king by then. As it turned out, King George refused even to look at their request.

John Adams

The son of a Massachusetts farmer, John Adams (1735–1826) became a successful lawyer and was urged into patriot activity by his cousin Samuel Adams. John became a tireless member of the Continental Congress and one of the strongest voices for revolution. Adams was a powerful speaker who loved a great debate; some called him honest and straightforward, while others said he was stubborn and vain. Adams was a member of the committee that drafted the Declaration of Independence, and it was he who proposed the creation of a continental army and nominated George Washington to be its commander. During the war, Adams helped to get aid for America from both France and Holland and helped negotiate the Treaty of Paris. He later served as ambassador to Great Britain, as vice president under George Washington, and then as president himself. Adams lived to see his eldest son become our sixth president before passing away on July 4, 1826—the fiftieth anniversary of the Declaration of Independence.

Patriot and President John Adams

Who fired the first shot of the American Revolution?
No one knows. Each side—the British Redcoats and the Massachusetts Minutemen (so named because they were said to be ready to pick up their guns on a minute's notice)—pointed the finger at the other.

The first shot of the revolution was fired in Lexington, Massachusetts, early on the morning of April 19, 1775. With tension rising in the colonies, Massachusetts patriots had begun stockpiling ammunition in the town of Concord, about eighteen miles outside Boston and about seven miles from Lexington. The British learned of the stash of munitions and set out to seize it. They also intended to seize Samuel Adams and John Hancock, whom they viewed as the patriot ringleaders. To save both the munitions and the men, Paul Revere kept watch over British movements around Boston. When he could tell

what the British were up to, he would take an early warning message to Lexington, where Adams and Hancock were hiding, and to Concord. Revere sent a spy to nose around the British and then relay a message from the steeple of Old North Church in Boston. The spy was to light one lantern if the Redcoats were coming by land, two if they were coming by sea.

When Revere heard that two lanterns were lit the night of April 18, he was off. He and another rider, William Dawes, took different routes to Lexington. They alerted every house with the message, "The Regulars are coming out!" (He didn't say, "The British are coming!" Most colonists still considered themselves British.) As they spread the news, about seventy Minutemen gathered on Lexington green to confront the Redcoats, who arrived early in the morning. The British troops, about 700 of them, were hoping to march right past the Minutemen. But an unordered shot rang out and both sides began firing. When the shooting stopped, eight Minutemen were dead.

The Redcoats marched on to Concord, where they found about 350 Minutemen waiting. Nearly 100 colonists were killed or wounded in the two battles. Between the battles and their return to Boston, the British suffered 250 dead or wounded.

Listen, my children, and you shall hear
Of the midnight ride of Paul Revere,
On the eighteenth of April, in Seventy-five,
Hardly a man is now alive
Who remembers that famous day and year.

No one knows why Henry Wadsworth Longfellow chose to immortalize only Paul Revere in "Paul Revere's Ride" (1860), his poem about that fateful April night, especially since Revere was captured before he completed his mission. (Perhaps "Revere" just fit Longfellow's rhyme scheme?) In any case, there were three riders carrying the message to Lexington and Concord—Revere, Dawes, and Dr. Samuel Prescott. Prescott joined Revere and Dawes just outside Lexington, but before the three could get on to Concord, they were stopped by a British patrol. It was Prescott who, since he knew the area well, managed to warn the people of Concord once they escaped.

AMERICAN ENGLISH

When you hear about Yankee Doodle going to town, do you ever wonder what a Yankee is, anyway? If so, you're not alone. No one knows for sure where the curious word *Yankee* comes from. People have suggested that it started with Indian words (but no such words have ever been found) or from the Dutch name *Jan Kees* (meaning, basically, John Cheese), or from a Dutch pirate named Yankey. Whatever its origin, it was not a complimentary term in colonial days. British officers used *Yankee* as a rude word for the Americans they disliked. American revolutionaries began to call themselves Yankees just to defy the British, and the name stuck. Today the rest of the world considers any American a Yankee. Within America the term has come to refer to a northerner, especially one from New England.

In 1775 did most colonists want to be independent from Britain?

No, believe it or not. Even though shots had been fired three weeks before, declaring independence from Britain was still a radical idea when the Second Continental Congress convened in May 1775. It was an entirely new concept for people anywhere to govern themselves—especially people who had been raised to revere English customs, royalty, and history. So despite the colonists' outrage at the taxes and unfair policies they'd been subjected to, most of them still hoped to reach a peaceful settlement with Britain.

In a last-ditch attempt to reconcile with King George, Congress wrote an "Olive Branch" petition. (An olive branch is a symbol of peace.) Meanwhile, Congress agreed to raise an army in case the petition failed, and elected the tall, dignified George Washington its commander in chief.

Six months later Congress learned that King George had again refused their petition. The king's snub, along with the publication of a little book called *Common Sense* in January 1776, pushed many colonists over the edge. By the beginning of summer, Congress was ready to formally declare independence from Great Britain.

In *Common Sense* author Thomas Paine (1737–1809) articulated what was . . . well, common sense, about the many reasons the colonies should be independent from Britain. The best-selling pamphlet said that monarchy was no good, that Britain's taxes and restrictions were bad for the American economy, and that it was silly for a tiny island to rule a continent three thousand miles away. An Englishman who came to America in 1774, Paine quickly became involved in the patriot cause. He took the things many colonists were feeling in their hearts about wanting to be free and put them into words. Paine also wrote a series of Revolutionary War–related pamphlets titled *The Crisis*, one of which started with the now-famous line "These are the times that try men's souls."

Thomas Jefferson

Writer and President Thomas Jefferson

Thomas Jefferson (1743–1826) was born into a life of wealth and privilege in Virginia, where his father taught him it was the duty of people in his social class to serve in government. Jefferson had broad interests and was always curious; he became not only a lawyer and politician but also an accomplished musician and self-taught architect, naturalist, and inventor. Tall, elegant, and cultured, Jefferson spoke six languages, founded the University of Virginia, and designed his own house, Monticello. After the Declaration of Independence was adopted, he spent many of the war years in Virginia politics. He then served as ambassador to France and went on to become our second vice president and third president of the United States. Though in public life he disliked pomp and circumstance, in his private life Jefferson had a weakness for finery that left him deeply in debt when he died. Like his friend (and sometime-foe) John Adams, Jefferson passed away on July 4, 1826.

You can tell what was most important to him in his life by the words he wrote for his tombstone. They don't mention the fact that he was president of the United States. Instead they say: "Here was buried Thomas Jefferson, author of the Declaration of American Independence, of the Statute of Virginia for Religious Freedom, and Father of the University of Virginia."

Why was Thomas Jefferson chosen to write the Declaration of Independence?

Thomas Jefferson, at age thirty-three one of the youngest delegates to the Second Continental Congress, was known to be an enlightened thinker and a talented writer. Congress appointed him to the committee to draft a declaration of independence, and his fellow committee members felt he was the best suited for the job. In just seventeen days, Jefferson produced an inspiring document that expressed the reasons for America's action and gave its soldiers and citizens an eloquent statement of what they were fighting for:

"We hold these Truths to be self-evident," Jefferson wrote, "that all Men are created equal, that they are endowed by their Creator with certain unalienable Rights, that among these are Life, Liberty, and the Pursuit of Happiness. . . ."

The Declaration of Independence states that a fair government recognizes and protects the rights of individuals, including life, liberty, and the pursuit of happiness. It also lists the wrongdoings of King George and Parliament, and says that because the king wouldn't listen to the colonists' complaints, the colonists were going to form a new, independent nation. Congress did edit Jefferson's draft (members ordered forty changes to his text, deleting 630 words and adding 146), but most of the words are his. The revised declaration was adopted on July 4, 1776.

Jefferson closed the document with the words, "And for the support of this Declaration . . . we mutually pledge to each other our Lives, our Fortunes and our sacred Honor." He wrote these words with utter seriousness, because the men who adopted and signed the Declaration of Independence were risking their lives. As British citizens, they could be tried and hanged for their treasonous actions.

The ideas about individual rights and freedom presented in the Declaration of Independence were not new ones, though they found a unique audience in America. The concepts came from a movement in Europe called the Enlightenment. Jefferson and other colonists read the works of the Enlightenment thinkers. That prompted them to read about the ancient democracies of Greece and Rome. The colonists realized that they could manage their own affairs—they'd been doing it since the House of Burgesses started in 1619, and they did it on their own farms. These brave, independent-minded people were prepared to act on Enlightenment ideals in a way no other people in the world could have at the time.

Whose name became another word for treason?

Benedict Arnold's. A brave soldier, Arnold (1741–1801) might have been an American hero if he hadn't become a traitor. In the early days of the war, Arnold was a bold commander who contributed to the important American victory at Saratoga. Yet he felt overlooked by his continental superiors and began to take bribes to spy for the British. After the Americans discovered that he had been part of a plot to capture the American fort at West Point, New York, Arnold fled and became a British officer who led vicious raids against the Americans. After the war he and his family were granted a royal pension and given land in Canada.

MAJOR MILESTONES IN THE AMERICAN REVOLUTION 1775–1783

1775

APRIL 19 The first shots of the American Revolution are fired as Redcoats pass through Lexington, Massachusetts.

JUNE 15 The Second Continental Congress votes to raise a continental army and appoints George Washington its commander. Washington accepts the job but refuses a salary.

JUNE 17 The first major battle of the war, the Battle of Bunker Hill, is actually fought at Breed's Hill just outside Boston.

1776

JANUARY 9 Thomas Paine publishes *Common Sense*.

JULY 2 The Continental Congress votes for independence.

JULY 4 The Continental Congress adopts the Declaration of Independence.

DECEMBER 25 Washington secretly leads troops across the Delaware River from Pennsylvania into New Jersey and surprises a camp of British forces at Trenton early the next morning. Washington's men kill 22, wound 92, and capture more than 900, losing none of their own army.

1777

SEPTEMBER 26 British General William Howe takes control of Philadelphia, which Congress had fled two weeks before.

OCTOBER 17 General John Burgoyne surrenders 5,700 British and hired German troops at Saratoga, New York. This significant American victory encourages Europeans to aid the revolution.

DECEMBER 17 Washington and his troops make winter quarters at Valley Forge, Pennsylvania. Of the 10,000 troops at Valley Forge, about 3,000 will die of starvation, disease, and exposure.

1778

FEBRUARY 6 Americans sign alliance treaty with France.

NOVEMBER 7 Congress passes the Articles of Confederation (though they were not adopted until 1781).

1779

SEPTEMBER 23 In the only major sea battle of the war, American Captain John Paul Jones captures the British warship *Serapis* off the coast of England. In one of the most famous exclamations of the revolution, Jones supposedly tells a British captain who asks for his surrender, "I have not yet begun to fight!"

1780

MAY 6 British capture Charleston, South Carolina, and take 5,400 Americans prisoner in the heaviest defeat of the war.

1781

OCTOBER 17 British Major General Lord Cornwallis sends a drummer boy to surrender to American and French forces at Yorktown, Virginia. Two days later the British soldiers give up their arms and officially surrender. Except for minor skirmishes that will follow, the war is effectively over.

1783

SEPTEMBER 3 British and American representatives sign the Treaty of Paris, officially ending the war and recognizing the United States of America as an independent nation.

Just whom did Jefferson mean when he wrote "all men are created equal"?

Did he mean women? Indians? Or blacks? We'll never know. Few people in Jefferson's time considered these people to be the equal of free white men. In Jefferson's draft of the declaration, he included a long section denouncing slavery as a "cruel war against human nature." But neither South Carolina nor Georgia, two major slave states, would sign the declaration unless that section was removed.

Yet despite Jefferson's opposition to slavery, he, and many of the men now called the Founders, did own slaves. It was a complex situation. Jefferson opposed slavery in theory, but in practice he knew he needed slaves to work his plantation. When it came time to establish the government for the new nation, no one could think of a practical way to solve this problem. So unfortunately the Founders wouldn't solve it at all. They would leave it for later generations to untangle.

AMERICAN VOICES

66 IN THE NEW CODE OF LAWS . . . I DESIRE YOU REMEMBER THE LADIES. . . . IF PARTICULAR CARE AND ATTENTION ARE NOT PAID TO THE LADIES WE ARE DETERMINED TO FOMENT A REBELLION AND WILL NOT HOLD OURSELVES BOUND BY ANY LAWS IN WHICH WE HAVE NO VOICE OR REPRESENTATION. 99

—ABIGAIL ADAMS (1744–1818) in a March 1776 letter to her husband, John Adams, who was attending the Second Continental Congress. Abigail Adams was a smart, strong, independent-minded woman who had been educated at home by her father. In a time when women had no voice or representation and were ruled by their fathers or husbands, Abigail often advised her husband in political matters.

Did blacks fight in the revolution?

They sure did. Some fought for the British. Early in the war, the British offered freedom to any slave who left his Patriot master to join their army. Tens of thousands of slaves ran away to take them up on their offer, though slaves of Loyalist masters were returned to their owners. By the end of the war, thousands of slaves had gained their freedom by fighting for the British.

On the American side, blacks fought bravely at Lexington and Concord and at Breed's Hill. At first Washington forbade the enlistment of black men. As the war continued, however, Washington and other commanders began to accept black men and boys into service. About five thousand black soldiers from every state except Georgia and South Carolina served in the Continental army during the war. Some were free blacks, but most were slaves. These soldiers changed many whites' minds about slavery. By the end of the war, Massachusetts and New Hampshire had abolished slavery, and Connecticut, Rhode Island, and Pennsylvania had adopted plans for gradual emancipation.

What roles did women and children play in the fight for independence?

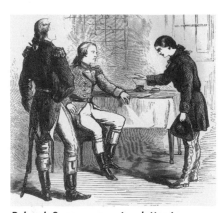

Deborah Samson presents a letter to General Washington.

At least one woman—Deborah Samson—disguised herself as a man and fought for a year and a half until she fell ill and doctors discovered she was a woman. As many as twenty thousand other women and children accompanied the army, cooking, washing, nursing, and helping keep camps clean. In some regiments there were as many wives and children as soldiers!

Just as important to the war effort was the home front, or the people who contributed to the cause from their homes instead of on the battlefield. Many women did things they'd never done before, running farms and businesses while their husbands were away. With their older children, they sewed clothes for soldiers, fed and cared for wounded troops who had fought near their homes, and helped make cartridges for muskets. Some even acted as unofficial spies.

Some young men, aged twelve to sixteen, enlisted in the army and became drummers or fifers (a *fife* is an instrument like a flute) to keep the soldiers marching in time. Many young boys also made good spies. Because they were small, they could slip in and out of small spaces and they weren't suspected by the British. Both boys and girls served as *couriers*, or messengers, who spread news and propaganda among groups of militia camped nearby. Young people knew the paths and backwoods areas around their homes very well, and some served as local guides for Continental army regiments—or offered their services to the British army and purposely got them lost or bogged down in a swamp! Sometimes these daring young patriots slashed the tops of British wagons or drilled holes in barrels to ruin the enemy's food supplies.

How did the colonists beat the best army in the world?

It was amazing that a small group of colonies would even try to go up against the British army. But the British had some major strikes against them. They were trying to control a war from three thousand miles away. They also underestimated the military ability of the rebels, who made up for their lack of soldiers, supplies, and experience by fighting in ways that were almost unheard-of at the time—ambushing, sniping, and deceiving.

But the major reason for the American victory was the French involvement in the war. Without French soldiers, money, and supplies—as much as 90 percent of the gunpowder used in the war came from France—the Americans could not have won. French King Louis XVI didn't believe in individual rights and freedom from monarchy (he was a king, after all), but he pitched in because he did like the idea of making England look bad. And, he figured, he might even get back some of the land his country lost in the French and Indian War. The American armies were also greatly helped by a nineteen-year-old French nobleman, the Marquis de Lafayette (1757–1834). Lafayette volunteered to serve in the colonial army at his own expense because he believed in the American cause. Lafayette fought well and bravely and became a general on George Washington's staff.

If buttercups buzzed after the bee;
If boats were on land, churches on sea;
If ponies rode men and grass ate cows;
And cats should be chased to holes by the mouse;
If the mammas sold their babies to the gypsies for half a crown;
Summer were spring and the t'other way round;
Then all the world would be upside down.

"The World Turned Upside Down" was a popular song of the revolutionary era. A British band played the tune as Major General Cornwallis's army surrendered at Yorktown on October 19, 1781. In many ways the world did seem upside down—a young colonial upstart had defeated a powerful and established European nation.

CHAPTER 3

Growth of a Nation

"Oh! say, does that star-spangled banner yet wave
O'er the land of the free and the home of the brave?"
—FRANCIS SCOTT KEY, *"The Star-Spangled Banner,"* 1814

Why did the United States go for eleven years without a president?

Because they weren't sure if they needed one. After they declared independence, members of the Continental Congress knew they needed to create some kind of government for the new nation. So they formed a *confederation*, or a loose association of almost-independent states. Under the Articles of Confederation, adopted in 1781, the states had more power than the national government. So at first there was no president. Nor were there any national courts. There was only Congress, and even it didn't have much power. Each state made its own laws, and eleven even had their own navies. Every state printed its own currency. So did Congress—so there were fourteen different kinds of money floating around!

What happened when delegates tried to improve the Articles of Confederation?

On May 25, 1787, fifty-five delegates from every state but Rhode Island met in Philadelphia to improve the Articles of Confederation. Yet instead of improving them, the delegates ended up scrapping them and starting all over again.

The Articles hadn't been very successful, but one important thing they did do was convince Americans that they wanted and needed a stronger national government. To create one, the delegates spent a long, hot summer in Philadelphia discussing, debating, and eventually hammering out the Constitution used today. When it was finished, the Constitution became a remarkable set of written rules that defined the power of the U.S. government and the rights of U.S. citizens.

These rules took a lot of compromising. The United States was already one of the biggest and most diverse countries in the world. There were lots of different interests to take into account, including those of northern states and southern states, small states and large states, slave states and free states. And once discussions got underway, people who had come together to fight for independence realized that they had very different ideas about what that independence meant. Who should have the power, and how much?

⭐ If Americans wanted to know how things were going at the Constitutional Convention during the summer of 1787, they were out of luck. The Framers (writers) of the Constitution had voted to keep their proceedings secret. They wanted to be able to change their minds about things they had already discussed, and they didn't want people tearing apart the Constitution before it was even finished. Despite the summer heat, the delegates kept all the windows of the Philadelphia State House closed when they worked on the first floor. They even posted watchmen to make sure nothing leaked out! Historians wouldn't know what happened if it weren't for James Madison, a delegate from Virginia, who took the most notes during the convention. Madison has been called the "Father of the Constitution" because of his leadership at the convention.

When was a human being only three-fifths of a person?

When he or she was a slave. This strange idea arose because of one of the biggest debates about the new government: representation in Congress. Should large states get more votes in Congress, or should every state have equal representation? The Virginia Plan, favored by large states, said that each state's population should determine the number of congressmen it got. The New Jersey Plan, favored by small states, said every state should have equal representation. Neither side would budge. Then Roger Sherman of Connecticut proposed a Great Compromise (also called the Connecticut Compromise). Sherman's solution was to have two houses in Congress, one with representation based on population (the House of Representatives), and another with equal representation of two members from each state (the Senate).

Then the question arose: How to count slaves in the population? Southern states didn't want the Constitution interfering with or stopping slavery. Yet at the same time, they wanted their slaves counted as part of a state's population when the time came to send representatives to Congress. It seemed they wanted the Constitution to ignore slaves, but to count them, too. The states that had already prohibited slavery were not going to let the slave states have it both ways. So there were more compromises. One was that Congress had to wait twenty years (until 1808) to pass any laws to control slavery. The other was that, for the purposes of deciding representation in the House, slaves would count as three-fifths of a person. (In other words, every five slaves would add three people to the state's population.) The delegates from northern states agreed to these compromises because slavery appeared to be dying out. They also wanted to preserve the union of states in the new nation, and the southern states wouldn't ratify, or approve, the Constitution without these changes.

What does our government have in common with a tightrope walker?

Without a lot of balance, both would come crashing down. The U.S. Constitution is the highest law in the land. It lays out the powers of the *federal*, or national, government and leaves the rest to the states. This is one balancing act. But the Framers also wanted to provide balance and power-sharing within the federal government. So they divided the government into three branches: the *legislative* branch, made up of the two houses of Congress, which makes the laws; the *executive* branch, headed by the president, which carries out the laws; and the *judicial* branch, headed by the Supreme Court, which reviews the laws and makes sure they are carried out in accordance with the Constitution. To keep one branch from having too much power, the Framers established a system of checks and balances. Each branch can "check" the others; for example, the president can veto a law passed by Congress. This maintains a balance among the three branches.

AMERICAN VOICES

66 WE THE PEOPLE OF THE UNITED STATES, IN ORDER TO FORM A MORE PERFECT UNION, ESTABLISH JUSTICE, ENSURE DOMESTIC TRANQUILITY, PROVIDE FOR THE COMMON DEFENCE, PROMOTE THE GENERAL WELFARE, AND SECURE THE BLESSINGS OF LIBERTY TO OURSELVES AND OUR POSTERITY, DO ORDAIN AND ESTABLISH THIS CONSTITUTION FOR THE UNITED STATES OF AMERICA. 99

—Preamble (introduction) to the U.S. Constitution

Who was "we" the people that the Constitution referred to?

Most historians say the Framers didn't mean all the people, but people like themselves—wealthy white farmers, merchants, and slave-owning planters. Under the Constitution, it was up to each state to determine which of its citizens could vote, hold office, and make laws. Some property ownership (usually less than had been required in colonial times) was the key qualification in almost every state. The idea was that if you had a lot of land, you probably also had an education and plenty of leisure time to read, think, and learn. But white male property owners were only about 25 percent of the total population. Women, blacks, American Indians, and poor whites were left out. Still, many more people were allowed to vote after the revolution than before it.

The Constitution wasn't perfect. But by the standards of the day, it was revolutionary. The Constitution gave more Americans more rights than any country had ever given its people. It's the oldest working constitution in the world, partly because it provides for its own *amendment*, or change. Some of the amendments we've made since 1787 have made "we the people" take in a much broader range of Americans.

> ★ Changing the Constitution is possible, but it's difficult enough that it can't be done on a whim. Of about ten thousand amendments that have been proposed in our history, only twenty-seven have made their way into the Constitution.

 The Constitution guarantees freedom of speech.

False. But the Bill of Rights does. Some states wouldn't ratify the Constitution unless rules were added to protect people's individual rights and keep the federal government from having too much power. The first ten amendments to the Constitution, called the Bill of Rights, guarantee basic liberties such as freedom of speech, freedom of the press, and freedom of religion. The Bill of Rights was ratified in 1791, three years after the Constitution went into effect.

Was ratification of the Constitution a "sure thing"?

No. Congress adopted the Constitution on September 17, 1787. But the Constitution had to be approved by at least nine of the thirteen states before it could go into effect. At this time, Americans were almost evenly split between those who favored the strong federal government of the Constitution (these people were soon called Federalists) and those who wanted a weaker federal government and stronger states' rights.

The first nine states to ratify the Constitution did not include Virginia and New York, two wealthy and influential states whose rejection would make the Constitution meaningless. The guarantee that the Bill of Rights would be added convinced Virginia to ratify. New York was partly persuaded by a series of eighty-five articles published in New York newspapers and then collected as *The Federalist Papers*. Most of the essays were written either by Alexander Hamilton, who was later secretary of the treasury, or James Madison, later president. *The Federalist Papers* said that the Constitution was the best way to protect the interests of all the people, allowing groups with different views to fight for their interests without harming the government. The *Papers* have become some of the most important documents in our history for their clear interpretation of the Constitution and the basis of our government.

At any rate, the Constitution was a go. The last two states, Rhode Island and North Carolina, ratified after the new government was already working and they'd seen the Bill of Rights.

Who elected George Washington as the first president?

A college. The electoral college, that is.

The United States has a curious way of electing its presidents. The Framers of the Constitution were wary of letting common people have a direct say in who led the country. They also worried that ordinary voters would not know of candidates outside their home states. So even though all voters can vote for president, the popular vote does not directly decide the election. Instead, each state elects a number of electors equal to its representation in Congress. Together the electors are called the electoral college. (A college is a place of higher learning, but it can also be a group of people who've come together with a common purpose.) Those electors actually vote for president. In most states whichever candidate gets the most popular votes gets all the states' electoral votes. In some states the electors must vote the way the majority of the voters in that state voted. But in other states electors can vote however they want (though they usually vote the way of the voters, anyway). Four times in American history—most recently in 2000—the winner of the popular vote has lost the electoral vote, and thus the election.

In 1789 every elector voted for George Washington. He was the only president in American history to be elected unanimously. When it came time for the president-elect to ride from his Virginia home to his inauguration in New York City, crowds of enthusiastic Americans met and cheered him all along the way.

AMERICAN VOICES

❝I WALK ON UNTRODDEN GROUND. THERE IS SCARCELY ANY PART OF MY CONDUCT WHICH MAY NOT HEREAFTER BE DRAWN INTO PRECEDENT.**❞**

—GEORGE WASHINGTON, *on beginning his presidency*

Why didn't Washington live in Washington, D.C.?

Because it wasn't built yet. When President Washington was *inaugurated*, or took the oath to become president, in 1789, the nation's temporary capital was New York City. In 1790 the temporary capital was moved to Philadelphia, and soon thereafter Washington set about choosing a new site for the permanent capital. Every state wanted the honor of having the capital city, so the solution was to build a federal city that wasn't part of any state at all. The new District of Columbia, carved out of Virginia and Maryland, would be in the middle of the country (the middle in 1790, that is).

The planning and building of the nation's capital began during Washington's presidency. Washington retired in 1797 after serving two terms. Just after Washington died in 1799, the nation's capital was named in his honor. Our second president, John Adams, moved into the still-unfinished White House (then called the President's House) in the still-unfinished city of Washington, D.C., in 1800.

AMERICAN PORTRAITS

Benjamin Banneker

Benjamin Banneker, born in 1731, was the son of slaves and grew up on a farm in Maryland. Though he learned to read and write, he had little education. Then, one day when he was twenty-one, he saw a remarkable thing: a pocket watch. The man who owned it lent it to him, and Benjamin took it apart and learned how it worked. Soon he had built a striking clock with parts he made himself. His interest in clocks led him to study mathematics and astronomy. He also learned to play the violin, wrote about natural history, and published an almanac. But perhaps his greatest contribution to history came when he was asked to survey the land for the nation's new capital. When Pierre L'Enfant, the city's architect, quit the job in a fit of temper, Banneker was able to re-create the plans from memory.

Although he was well respected as a scientist, Banneker never lost sight of the fact that his skin color blocked him from the basic rights of other American citizens. In 1791 he wrote a letter to Thomas Jefferson, who was then secretary of state. Sending Jefferson a copy of his almanac, he said what few had dared to say: that the man who wrote "all men are created equal" himself held slaves. "[How] pitiable is it to reflect," he wrote, "that . . . you should at the same time be found guilty of that most criminal act, which you professedly detested in others." Jefferson replied. "No body wishes more than I do," he said, "to see such proofs as you exhibit, that nature has given to our black brethren talents equal to those of the other colors of men." He did not, however, free his slaves.

Was the "Revolution of 1800" another bloody war?

No. In fact, it wasn't a war at all. It was a transfer of power between political rivals. During George Washington's presidency, people began to form political parties—groups with particular ideas about how the government should be run. Tension between the political parties heated up during John Adams's term. Even Thomas Jefferson, Adams's own vice president, took sides against him.

Jefferson had actually run against Adams in the election of 1796. He came in a close second, and because of the way elections were conducted at the time, he became vice president. (Since the Framers hadn't foreseen the rise of political parties, electors voted for one of two candidates and the one with the most votes became president, the one with the second most, vice president. That meant that the president and vice president could be political enemies. In 1804 the Twelfth Amendment to the Constitution fixed this problem by establishing separate voting for the offices of president and vice president, with each pair of candidates from the same party.)

Jefferson spent most of his term as vice president at home in Virginia because he disagreed with Adams. In 1800 he ran against Adams again and beat him. Jefferson called his election as the nation's third president a revolution because he felt his ideas about government were so different from those of Washington and Adams. He wanted to cut the size and power of the young federal government. And Jefferson meant to be a man of the people, an ordinary man like all those he trusted to govern themselves. On the day of his inauguration, President-elect Jefferson dressed in a plain gray vest and green breeches and walked the two blocks from his Washington boardinghouse to the Capitol building.

Jefferson's election was a revolution of sorts, though he wouldn't change things as much as he thought he did. Perhaps most importantly, his inauguration was the first time in modern world history that power passed peacefully between political rivals. It was a good sign for the future of the United States and its democratic process.

How did the United States get twice as big, overnight?

In May 1803 two of President Jefferson's advisors bought the Louisiana Territory, land that stretched from the Mississippi River west to the Rocky Mountains, from French dictator Napoléon Bonaparte. France had just regained the territory from Spain, which had held it since the end of the French and Indian War. The Louisiana Purchase doubled the size of the United States.

The enormous land deal surprised Americans, the president included. Jefferson had asked James Monroe to join Robert Livingston in France and ask Napoléon if he would sell New Orleans to the United States. Livingston and Monroe were shocked when Napoléon offered to sell all of France's territory in America. He was fighting wars in Europe, and he needed money more than he needed land across the ocean. The total price was $15 million, or about four cents an acre. It was a bargain. Most Americans overwhelmingly approved of the Louisiana Purchase, even if some thought it was extravagant. The vast territory eventually became all or part of fifteen states.

SETTING IT STRAIGHT

Did the Louisiana Purchase spark the Lewis and Clark Expedition?

No. Even before the Louisiana Purchase, President Jefferson had been organizing an expedition to travel to the Pacific Ocean. Few Americans in the East knew much about the West, and Jefferson was curious. The Louisiana Purchase only made him more so. The president told the leaders of the "Corps of Discovery," Meriwether Lewis (1774–1809) and his cocaptain, William Clark (1770–1838), to make careful scientific records of the land, plants, and animals they saw; to make peaceful contact with any Indians they met; and especially to look for a Northwest Passage, an all-water route to the Pacific. At their

winter camp in present-day North Dakota, Lewis and Clark met a Shoshone Indian girl named Sacagawea. Sacagawea joined the expedition with her French husband in the spring. Without her help as a guide and interpreter, and especially without the horses she helped the Corps obtain, Lewis and Clark might never have made it to the Pacific.

It seems strange today, but Lewis and Clark knew less about their destination than the first astronauts did about the moon—at least the astronauts had pictures! The Corps of Discovery traveled eight thousand miles through unmapped and often dangerous territory. The group was gone twenty-eight months and lost only one man (to appendicitis). Though Lewis and Clark never found a Northwest Passage, they did return with hundreds of plant and animal samples and a wealth of information. They also aroused the interest of Americans, who were increasingly looking westward.

AMERICAN VOICES

❝WE WERE ABOUT TO PENETRATE A COUNTRY AT LEAST TWO THOUSAND MILES IN WIDTH, ON WHICH THE FOOT OF CIVILIZED MAN HAD NEVER TRODDEN; THE GOOD OR EVIL IT HAD IN STORE FOR US WAS FOR EXPERIMENT YET TO DETERMINE.❞

—*From the journal of* MERIWETHER LEWIS, *April 7, 1805*

Who were Tecumseh and "the Prophet"?

Tecumseh was a young Shawnee chief who lived in the Ohio River valley. As thousands of white settlers spilled west across the Appalachian Mountains, the U.S. government made countless treaties with the Indians to take over as much of their tribal lands as possible. Tecumseh refused to sign any treaties and instead organized a resistance movement against the whites' invasion. He dreamed of a huge Indian confederacy whose strength would keep whites from moving farther west.

Shawnee chief Tecumseh

Tecumseh and his brother Tenskwatawa, "the Prophet," a wise and respected religious leader, traveled to tribes from Wisconsin to Florida. The Prophet spoke about restoring Indian pride and customs while Tecumseh drummed up support for his confederacy.

The confederation scared U.S. authorities, particularly General William Henry Harrison, governor of the Indiana Territory (and a future president). In 1811, while Tecumseh was away recruiting more warriors, Harrison's army defeated fighters led by the Prophet at the Tippecanoe River. The defeat discredited the Prophet, who had told the braves that the Americans' bullets would bounce off their chests. (Of course, they didn't.) Tecumseh tried to save his crumbling alliance by teaming up with the British in Canada and in forts west of the Appalachians. The British helped and supplied the Indians with weapons—and outraged the Americans.

Was Johnny Appleseed a real man?

You bet your apples he was! Unlike stories about many American folk heroes, a good portion of the tales about John Chapman (1774–1845), better known as Johnny Appleseed, may actually be true. No one knows much about Johnny's early years, except that he was born near Leominster, Massachusetts, and grew up to be a skilled nurseryman. Johnny spent his adult life traveling through Pennsylvania, Ohio, Michigan, Indiana, and Illinois, planting apple orchards and selling seedlings to pioneers who were carving homes out of the wilderness. Known for his generous and peaceful ways, Johnny often visited a newcomer's home with a handful of medicinal herbs in his hand. Though Johnny never married, he especially loved children and was a welcome guest and storyteller at many a settler's cabin.

Johnny Appleseed never carried a gun, knife, or weapon of any kind. He was a deeply religious man who lived in harmony with nature, wild animals, Indians, and white settlers alike. He spent most of his time outdoors, and it's likely that he went barefoot much of the time. (It's said that he could walk over ice and snow in the coldest weather, the skin on his feet was so tough!) It's not likely that he wore a cooking pan on his head, as he is often pictured, though he almost certainly carried one tied onto his pack.

No one knows how far Johnny's planting extended, or how many seedlings grown from the fruit of his trees were taken elsewhere. So anywhere in the United States, people may wonder whether a particular apple tree came from seeds sown by Johnny Appleseed.

What was "the second American Revolution"?

The War of 1812, which made Britain realize that its American colonies were gone forever. The United States was tired of the British interfering in American affairs and acting like the former colonies would be theirs again one day. And if the

United States could push the British out of Canada, that would mean more territory for land-hungry westerners. Americans also had their eyes on Florida (held by Spain, Britain's ally). "War hawks," who were itching to fight for these lands, pushed President James Madison into war with Great Britain.

The war, which was fought from 1812 to 1815, had been brewing on the seas as well as in the west. In 1812 war was still raging between England and France. Both the British and the French had been capturing American ships and taking sailors prisoner, but the British forced the captured sailors to work for them. (This was called *impressment* into the Royal Navy.) Impressment just added fuel to the war hawks' fire.

In 1812 the young United States was sorely unprepared for war. Despite an inadequate army and navy, some Americans thought victory would be easy since the British were preoccupied with Napoléon's armies in Europe. The United States did have some early victories in Canada, but they didn't have the upper hand for long. When the Napoleonic Wars ended in 1814, the British sent boatloads of troops to the United States. Those troops wasted little time marching on Washington, D.C., and setting the White House, the Capitol, and several other government buildings ablaze. The president's wife, First Lady Dolley Madison, is famous for not fleeing the White House until a famous portrait of George Washington was removed from the wall and taken to safety.

What did America gain from the War of 1812?

a) respect and national pride

b) words to our national anthem

c) not much

d) all of the above

The answer is letter d. Neither side gained much from the War of 1812. After three years of fighting, the Treaty of Ghent pretty much returned things to the way they'd been before the war. The Treaty of Ghent, signed in Belgium in 1815, set boundaries between the United States and Canada and put the Oregon Territory in the Pacific Northwest under joint control. Americans had learned they couldn't have Canada, and the British learned that they couldn't have America back. Knowing they had held their own against powerful Britain, not once but twice, gave Americans respect and national pride.

Americans also took pride in the hero they found in General Andrew Jackson. In the last major contest of the war, the Battle of New Orleans, Jackson won an impressive victory. The British lost more than two thousand soldiers, the Americans, eight. The battle had no impact on the outcome of the war because it was fought after the Treaty of Ghent had restored peace. (The news hadn't made its way across the ocean yet.) But Jackson became a national hero anyway. Fewer than fifteen years later, he was president.

The war also gave the country the song that would become the national anthem. After British troops burned Washington, they moved on to Baltimore and bombarded Fort McHenry. There, a lawyer named Francis Scott Key was held on a British warship in Baltimore Harbor. As he watched the "rockets' red glare" and the "bombs bursting in air" during the twenty-five-hour siege, Key kept his eye on the enormous American flag that flew above Fort McHenry. He knew that as long as the stars and stripes waved, the Americans had not been defeated. Inspired, Key wrote the poem "Defense of Fort McHenry," which became the words to "The Star-Spangled Banner."

Defense of Fort McHenry

Oh, say, can you see, by the dawn's early light,
What so proudly we hail'd at the twilight's last gleaming?
Whose broad stripes and bright stars, thro' the perilous fight,
O'er the ramparts we watch'd, were so gallantly streaming?
And the rockets' red glare, the bombs bursting in air,
Gave proof thro' the night that our flag was still there.
O say, does that star-spangled banner yet wave
O'er the land of the free and the home of the brave?

How did the United States gain Florida?

The United States didn't win it in the War of 1812, but that didn't mean Americans—or General Andrew Jackson—had forgotten about it. During the War of 1812, Jackson became known for his particularly ruthless fighting against Creek Indians in the South. In 1817 President James Monroe asked Jackson to look into raids made on Georgia settlements by Florida's Seminole Indians and the runaway slaves who lived with the Seminoles. Spain still held Florida, and Jackson didn't have permission to invade Spanish territory. But he invaded anyway, burning villages and crops and overthrowing the Spanish governor. Spain was too weak to fight a war, so in 1819 it sold Florida to the United States for $5 million. (Spain still held Texas, California, and the Southwest.) Jackson became governor of the Florida Territory.

Why did President Monroe tell Europe to "keep out"?

After the War of 1812, the United States seemed to have a new confidence. There was finally peace in Europe, and in politics at home. The American economy began to hum, as machines and inventions created new products, jobs, and opportunities. For these reasons James Monroe's years as president have been called the "Era of Good Feelings."

To keep these "Good Feelings" from going sour, Monroe gave a speech in 1823 that came to be known as the Monroe Doctrine. In his speech President Monroe said that the Americas—North, South, and Central—were off limits to European nations. He said the United States would not tolerate Europeans looking for colonies in the Americas; in return, the United States would not interfere in European affairs. (Basically Monroe said, "Keep out and we will, too.") Monroe's speech was motivated by the Spanish and Portuguese colonies in South America that were declaring independence from their mother countries, just as the Americans had done nearly fifty years before. Other European nations were looking to claim the former colonies, but President Monroe wouldn't have it. He wanted the United States to be the only major power in the Americas.

★ One reason Spain was too weak to fight for Florida was that, since 1810, it had been battling a series of rebellions in Mexico. When Mexico finally won its independence in 1821, Spain granted Mexico all its land in North America. Mexico's new government was weak and unstable. It invited American merchants and settlers into parts of its territory, including New Mexico and Texas—not realizing Americans would establish a foothold they would never relinquish.

AMERICAN ENGLISH

American pride found its way into American spelling, helped mainly by the stubborn patriot and dictionary maker Noah Webster. "America must be as independent in literature as she is in politics," he wrote, and for him that included freedom from British spelling. In dictionaries that Webster created in the early nineteenth century, he boldly introduced simpler, Americanized spellings. *Colour* became *color, theatre* changed to *theater, travelling* to *traveling*. Some of his changes—such as *tongue* to *tung*—didn't stick, but many of them persist to this day, marking one more difference between American English and British English.

CHAPTER 4

The Way West

"Go west, young man, go west, and grow up with the land."

—Nineteenth-century newspaper editor JOHN SOULE, often quoted by fellow journalist Horace Greeley

What was the main reason Maine became a state?

Slavery. But not slavery in Maine, slavery in Missouri. Here's the story:

In 1819 the Missouri Territory petitioned for statehood. At that time the nation had eleven free states and eleven slave states. When Missouri asked to enter the Union as a slave state, northern congressmen erupted in protest. The addition of Missouri would give the slave states more votes in the Senate. The northerners proposed that slavery be abolished in Missouri. That made southerners angry and set off a long and ugly debate in Congress.

Senator Henry Clay of Kentucky, known as the "Great Compromiser," came up with a solution that allowed Missouri to enter as a slave state. But it also admitted Maine, which had just separated from Massachusetts, as a free state. That maintained the balance in the Senate. The Compromise also divided the Louisiana Territory at 36°30' on the map. All territories north of that line and west of the Mississippi would be free, the rest slave.

The Missouri Compromise, approved in 1820, was clearly only a temporary solution. The gap between Americans who favored slavery and those who didn't was getting wider.

What helped keep slavery going in the South?

When the Framers wrote the Constitution, slavery had been limping to an end. Tobacco had worn out the soil in the South and there wasn't much for slaves to do. Factories in England and New England had great demand for cotton, but still it was hard to make money growing it because it had to be seeded, a very time-consuming task. But after a man named Eli Whitney improved the cotton gin (*gin* was short for "engine") in 1793, a worker could remove the seeds from fifty times more cotton— fifty pounds instead of just one pound—each day. Suddenly growing a lot of cotton could make you very rich. Southern planters clamored for land and for inexpensive labor to pick, bale (wrap), and clean their crop. "King Cotton" came to rule the South, and slavery flourished instead of faded. Between 1820 and 1850, the number of slaves in this country doubled to 3 million. Though the slave trade had been banned in 1808, the slave population increased because slaves were smuggled into the country and existing slaves had children.

How did Andrew Jackson change the presidency, before he even stepped into the White House?

He got elected. Unlike all the privileged Virginians and Massachusetts men who had preceded him as president, Andrew Jackson (1767–1845) was born to a poor family in a log cabin in South Carolina. His father died before he was born; his mother passed away when he was fourteen. Andrew had very little schooling, but he learned to read, something many adults on the frontier couldn't do in his day.

Jackson joined the Continental army as an orderly when he was only thirteen. He was a hot-tempered young man who gambled, played practical jokes, and even killed a man in a duel. He went on to become a successful lawyer, congressman, military general, landowner, and slave owner. Though he never really got rid of his hot temper, he did mellow as he got older. His admirers called him "Old Hickory" because he was as tough as a hickory tree.

By the time Jackson ran for president in 1828, the nation was not what it had been at the beginning. There were more states (a total of twenty-four) and about three times as many people, many of whom were pushing west. They were opening new frontiers and making their own way, and more democratic ways of government seemed in order. Jackson was the symbol of the self-made frontiersman. If he could become president, anyone could. (Well, any white male, that is.) His election meant the opening of the political process to more people as western states abandoned property ownership as a requirement for voting. The changes in government Jackson represented became known as Jacksonian democracy.

> ★ Ordinary citizens from all over the country came to see their hero Andy Jackson sworn in as president of the United States. After Jackson's inauguration, frontiersmen in buckskin and muddy boots streamed into the White House, climbing through doors and windows and on top of satin chairs and fine tables. They spilled punch and broke glass and pushed and shoved one another. President Jackson had to be let out of the rowdy party through a window!

Andrew Jackson was the first president to ride on a

a) horse   c) scooter   e) camel

b) train   d) snowboard

The answer is letter *b*. As America grew, so did its need for efficient transportation. Trains were just one of the new ways for people, goods, and raw materials like iron and coal to travel around the country.

Before the railroads, when the only roads America knew were bumpy dirt trails, travel over land was difficult, dangerous, and slow. It was usually safer and faster to go by water—especially after inventor Robert Fulton used steam power to create America's first commercially successful steamboat. These vessels were faster than boats powered by sails or oars, especially when going against the current. Canals, such as the Erie Canal, which in 1825 connected the Hudson River in New

York to the Great Lakes, also made it easier to move people and goods long distances by water.

Tom Thumb, built by Peter Cooper

But travel by water was never as popular as travel by railroads would be. When the nation's first passenger railroad, the Baltimore & Ohio, opened in 1828, horses pulled the cars along the track. Soon, however, America's first steam-powered locomotive, named *Tom Thumb* because it was so small, chugged along the Baltimore & Ohio track. Over the following decades, workers laid thousands of miles of track for the "Iron Horse," or locomotive, connecting the nation as nothing before it had.

Were trains the only things going lickety-split in America?

No. So many other things were moving quickly that better trains were needed. Most significantly, new technology was beginning to make America an industrial nation.

In colonial times Americans usually either made their goods at home or imported them from overseas. Not long after the American Revolution, the British began producing goods in factories. This was the beginning of another kind of revolution—the Industrial Revolution. It combined new inventions and machines with new ways of organizing workers to make goods faster, cheaper, and often better than at home.

The British wanted to keep the mechanics of their factories a secret. But American businessmen were offering rewards to anyone who could build a British-style factory. A young factory apprentice named Samuel Slater memorized everything he saw at work, then disguised himself and sailed to America. In 1790 Slater built a water-powered mill that spun wool into yarn next to a river in Pawtucket, Rhode Island. Soon there were mills along many New England rivers (thus the growing demand for cotton). About twenty years later, a man named Francis Cabot Lowell opened a mill in Massachusetts. It was the first factory in the world to combine spinning and weaving and to turn raw cotton into finished fabric.

Textile mills were only one kind of factory. Each new idea or invention sparked another one, and soon factories made shoes, farm equipment, iron, and lots of other things. By 1851 the Industrial Revolution was full steam ahead in America, and more and more Americans were buying American products.

Was the Industrial Revolution good for all Americans?

The Industrial Revolution did do a lot of good things, like making our nation stronger and allowing more Americans to afford more things because many goods became less expensive. For some workers the Industrial Revolution brought an escape from poverty. But for many of them, the pay was low, the hours long, and the work mind-numbing and often dangerous. Once steam power came into use, factories did not have to rely on river power and could be built in cities. Cities grew to take in the new workers, and soon they were dirty and overcrowded places where many people lived in cramped boardinghouses. These surroundings were very different from the small farming communities most people had known. Workers feared losing their jobs. A growing population meant there was always a steady pool of workers, and employers could keep wages low.

The Industrial Revolution also changed the nation as a whole. The factories were built in the North, where the land was not good for farming. Thus the North became more industrial and demanded more cotton from the South, which in turn kept the South agricultural. It was easier and more profitable for the South to go on growing cotton with slave labor than it was to build factories. The North and South had always had their differences, but now the two regions were becoming two separate nations with different economies and interests.

The first factory workers in America were children.

True. Sam Slater's mill opened with nine workers, all of them under the age of twelve. By the 1800s nearly half the nation's textile workers were under ten years of age and were working twelve or more hours a day. Many children, some as young as six or seven, worked in factories to earn badly needed money for their families. Employers hired them because of their small, quick hands and their ability to get under and inside machines to clean them. They were more obedient than adults and, most importantly, they could be paid less. One man who worked in a Rhode Island cotton mill as a child figured out that he was making seven cents a day, or half a cent an hour.

Industry was booming in the Northeast. What was happening in the South?

President Andrew Jackson and Congress were working to gain territory that belonged to Indians. As a general, Jackson had fought both with and against Indians, and he knew their culture better than most Americans. But he also wanted their land for white Americans.

In 1830 Congress passed the Indian Removal Act. The act forced Indians living east of the Mississippi River to move west to Indian Territory set aside for them. The government concentrated on the Choctaw, Chickasaw, Creek, Seminole, and Cherokee of the Southeast. These were the "Five Civilized Tribes," so called because they had adopted many of the white settlers' ways. They farmed and kept slaves, and many had converted to Christianity. The Cherokees also had their own system of representational government and had established an independent Cherokee Nation. Even though this sort of "civilization" was what the U.S. government encouraged for Indians, these tribes also lived smack in the middle of prime cotton-growing land—land that white Southerners wanted. On top of that, gold was found on Cherokee land in 1828. Of course, white settlers wanted that, too.

Cherokee leader John Ross traveled to Washington to ask the Supreme Court to let his people keep their land. And he won. Chief Justice John Marshall ruled that the Cherokee Nation was not subject to the laws of the United States and did have a right to its own land. Yet the Cherokee had to move west anyway. Why? Because President Jackson refused to enforce the law. So the Indians were forced west on the "Trail Where They Cried," also known as the Trail of Tears.

Cherokees were almost the last to go, starting in 1838. Soldiers dragged young and old from their homes with only the clothes on their backs. They herded them together and marched them, at bayonet point and through all kinds of weather, from their lush, sacred homelands in Georgia and surrounding states to land that is now Oklahoma. Often there was not enough food or shelter on the journey, and four thousand Cherokees—or one in every four who marched—died of cold or starvation on the way. Years later, looking back on the Trail of Tears, one soldier-escort remarked, "I fought through the Civil War, and have seen men shot to pieces and slaughtered by thousands, but the Cherokee removal was the cruelest work I ever knew."

 Most tribes who resisted removal to the West didn't do so in the Supreme Court but in fierce battles against the U.S. army. In the Midwest, Chief Black Hawk of the Sauk and Fox tribes had agreed to move from Illinois across the Mississippi to Iowa. Yet the hunting in Iowa was so poor that Black Hawk returned to Illinois to farm. When 1,000 of his warriors tried to surrender to the U.S. army in 1832, all but 150 were shot down. Black Hawk was captured.

Even stronger resistance came from the Seminoles, one of the five civilized tribes, and their young warrior leader Osceola. Osceola fought the U.S. army brilliantly and stealthily from the swamps of Florida. He was finally captured not by military might but with a trick. When the Seminoles raised the white flag of truce in 1837, the U.S. army seized their leader. Imprisoned, Osceola died in 1838. Though most Americans supported President Jackson's policy of Indian Removal, they were outraged at this disgraceful violation of the rules of war.

Who was Nat Turner, and on whom did he turn?

A woodcut showing tragic scenes from the rebellion

Nat Turner was a Virginia slave who led a band of about seventy other slaves in a violent rebellion in 1831. Just before dawn on August 22, the small army of slaves killed Turner's masters and went on to murder every white person they met in the next twenty-four hours. About sixty whites were dead before Turner went into hiding. For two months, the South was in a state of panic while thousands of soldiers looked for him. Before Turner was captured in October, whites went on a rampage of their own, killing any slave even remotely suspected of having anything to do with the rebellion.

Nat Turner's revolt was not the first slave rebellion, nor the first to fail. But it was the first to provoke such panic in the South. Even after Turner was hanged, many whites feared his influence. New, stricter laws made slavery even more brutal than before. Southern states restricted the education of slaves and made it harder to free them or to speak out against slavery.

Sequoyah

Born to a Cherokee mother and white father in Tennessee around 1776, Sequoyah grew up lame, brilliant, and illiterate. No Cherokee could read or write his or her own language, for the simple reason that there was no written Cherokee. Sequoyah would change that.

Although he was by trade a silversmith, Sequoyah became fascinated with English writing. So he set out to create a system of writing for the Cherokees, too, comparing the task to "catching a wild animal and taming it." Eventually he came up with a script in which eighty-six symbols represented eighty-six spoken syllables in the Cherokee language. It was so logical and easy that most people learned to read it within weeks. To this day the Cherokee script is considered an amazing accomplishment. It is the only system of writing invented independently by a single person and actually used by a nation.

Equipped with a written language, the Cherokee Nation soon produced an influential newspaper, the *Cherokee Phoenix*, and wrote its own constitution. Sequoyah became a hero for giving a voice to his people.

Having a low opinion of white people and their false promises, Sequoyah moved west years before the sad events of the Trail of Tears. In 1905, sixty-two years after his death in Texas, Indians in the West tried to form a new state called Sequoyah. They failed (it became Oklahoma instead), but Sequoyah's name lives on in everything from a county in Oklahoma to the beautiful giant redwood tree of the West.

What happened at the Alamo?

The Alamo was a former church building and military post in San Antonio, Texas. It became part of American history in 1836, when a battle broke out there between Mexicans and Texans.

Texas was then part of Mexico, but thousands of Americans had bought land there on the invitation of the Mexican government. By 1830 there were more than 20,000 white Americans and 2,000 of their slaves in Texas. Americans quickly outnumbered Mexicans, and in 1834 the Americans asked Mexican leaders to allow Texas to separate from Mexico. The Americans had two motives: They wanted to remain American, to be sure, but they also wanted to keep their slaves. (Mexico had already stopped slavery.)

Mexican leader General Antonio López de Santa Anna denied the Americans' request, so in 1835 the Americans announced that they would declare Texas's independence from Mexico. The angry Santa Anna marched 3,000 troops to San Antonio. There, about 180 men, including the well-known frontiersmen Davy Crockett and Jim Bowie, waited inside the Alamo. They managed to fend off Santa Anna's troops for thirteen days until March 6, 1836, but the numbers against them were just too great. The only Americans to come out of the Alamo alive were a woman, her baby, and a slave. Santa Anna spared these three so they could warn Sam Houston, the commander of the Texas army, what awaited him.

On March 27, 1836, Americans forces were again overcome at a town called Goliad. But soon thereafter they defeated Santa Anna in a swift battle at San Jacinto, where Sam Houston rallied his troops with the battle cry "Remember the Alamo!" Texas became an independent country and then asked to join the United States. Neither President Jackson, nor his successor, Martin Van Buren, would admit Texas to the Union. Both feared that doing so would start a war with Mexico. It would also upset the balance of free states and slave states that had been reached under the Missouri Compromise. Texas remained the "Lone Star Republic" for nine years before it became a state in 1845.

By the time President Van Buren (1782–1862), a Democrat like Andrew Jackson, ran for reelection in 1840, the ideal of the American as frontier hero had taken over the American imagination. The Whig Party opposed Van Buren by saying that their candidate, William Henry Harrison (who had lost to Van Buren in 1836), was a plain man of the people—even though he was really a Virginia aristocrat who lived in a mansion. The Whigs used buttons, posters, songs, rallies, and slogans (all things people connect with modern political campaigns) to make the election famous as the "log cabin and cider" campaign. Saying Harrison lived in a log cabin and preferred hard cider to fancy wine was meant to show that Harrison was a common man. The image-crafting worked this time. Harrison beat Van Buren decisively.

After all that campaigning, Harrison served as president for only a month before he died of pneumonia (which he caught giving a two-hour inaugural address in the rain). Upon Harrison's death, John Tyler became the first vice president to assume the presidency. People called Tyler "His Accidency," and many thought he would just serve as caretaker until the next election. But Tyler became a full-fledged president, setting the example for all the vice presidents who would take over the presidency after him.

Did "Oregon Fever" keep you in bed for days?

It wasn't a disease, but an overpowering desire to pick up and move west. Americans "caught" Oregon Fever from rumors, letters, or newspaper articles—anything that told of Oregon's beauty and riches.

Since colonial days, settlers had pushed farther and farther west into wilderness that had long been home to Indians. After Lewis and Clark's expedition, trappers and traders went west to hunt beaver and other wildlife that filled the rivers and forests. A handful of missionaries followed these mountain men into the wild and went to live among the Indians, hoping to convert them to Christianity. The missionaries' letters drifted back east, convincing Americans that the West wasn't just a place for rugged individuals but a land of gentle climate, fresh streams, and rich farmland waiting for anyone willing to make the journey.

The West also seemed to be a land of hope, freedom, and opportunity at a time when many Americans were looking for a fresh start. By the 1830s eastern cities were dirty, crowded, and disease-ridden. To many Americans who wished to make a better life for themselves, the difficult and dangerous journey seemed worth it.

⭐ One promoter described the Oregon Territory as a paradise where "the pigs are running about under the great acorn trees, round and fat, and already cooked, with knives and forks sticking in them so that you can cut off a slice whenever you are hungry." No wonder people caught Oregon Fever!

How did the pioneers know where to go?

Mountain men and traders blazed and mapped several old Indian routes for settlers to follow. Among the trails were the Santa Fe, the California, the Gila, the Old Spanish, the Mormon, and the most famous and well-traveled of them all, the Oregon Trail. In 1841, the year the first wagon trains traveled the Oregon Trail, a hundred pioneer families loaded their covered wagons and set out for Oregon and California. In 1843 a thousand more did the same; and over the next fifty years, hundreds of thousands.

Oregon Fever didn't seem to be dampened by the fact that, at least in the beginning, the pioneers' destinations weren't part

On the Oregon Trail by William Henry Jackson

of the United States. (The Oregon Territory was jointly held by the United States and Great Britain, and California and the Southwest were part of Mexico.) The first settlers were actually *emigrants*, or people leaving their country for another, though most were confident that the United States would catch up with them sooner or later. The belief that America would one day stretch from sea to shining sea was partly due to the writings of a journalist named John O'Sullivan, who wrote in 1845 of America's "manifest destiny to overspread the continent allotted by Providence for the free development of our yearly multiplying millions." To some, this "Manifest Destiny" was the heroic taming and peopling of the West; to others—the Indians—it was the unpeopling of it.

★ The telegraph, invented by Samuel Morse in 1837, helped to keep pioneers connected to life back home. The device could send messages over wires almost instantaneously using electrical current and the dots and dashes of Morse Code. Without the telegraph, the United States might not have been able to exist over such an expanse of territory and still be unified by a single government. By 1851 telegraph cable connected major U.S. cities, and by 1861 it connected the two coasts.

When is a shortcut not a shortcut?

When it makes your journey longer instead of shorter. For pioneers making the journey west, this could be deadly. One of the worst disaster stories of the westward migration involved the Donner party, a group of settlers who in 1846 took a shortcut recommended by their guidebook. The book's author had never actually taken the shortcut himself. The route left the travelers stranded along the California Trail when snow from an early winter storm sealed their pass through the Sierra Nevada. Starving, the party chewed on animal bones and hides, twigs, and even their shoes. Finally, as people died, the survivors ate the bodies of their dead comrades to stay alive. A few survivors climbed a mountain to find help. When rescuers arrived, only forty-six of the original eighty-seven were alive.

What did President James K. Polk do that no president had done before him?

He governed a United States that stretched from coast to coast. After President Polk settled an argument with Britain about the U.S.-Canadian border, the United States got the land that is now Oregon and Washington.

John Tyler, the president before Polk, admitted Texas as a state on his last day in office, setting off the Mexican War (1846–1848). Polk, a firm believer in Manifest Destiny, sent troops into Texas because he said the southern boundary of Texas was the Rio Grande. Mexico, however, said it was the Nueces River, farther north. Ulysses S. Grant, who fought in the war and would later become president of the United States, said the Mexican War was "one of the most unjust ever waged by a stronger against a weaker nation." It was an aggressive war for expansion that the United States won relatively easily.

The Mexican War ended in the Treaty of Guadalupe Hidalgo, which fixed the Texas border at the Rio Grande and gave the United States all of California, Nevada, Utah, and parts of Arizona, New Mexico, Colorado, and Wyoming for $15 million. Five years later, the United States paid Mexico another $10 million for a strip of land in southern New Mexico and Arizona called the Gadsden Purchase. Winning the war gave the United States territory from Atlantic to Pacific, but it also created more land in which the slavery problem would have to be dealt with.

★ Land wasn't the only thing the United States gained in the Treaty of Guadalupe Hidalgo—it also gained tens of thousands of new citizens. Hispanics living in the formerly Mexican territory were given the choice of becoming U.S. citizens or moving to Mexico. Many of them were descendants of Mexicans, Indians, or Spanish missionaries who had settled in the region generations earlier, and most chose to stay. Even though the Hispanics had been there longer, Americans who moved into the area did not hesitate to force the Hispanics off their land and into low-paying jobs. Despite the discrimination they faced, Hispanics held on to their heritage and culture, both of which remain an important part of the American Southwest today.

Who were the forty-niners before they were San Francisco's football team?

They were the thousands upon thousands of gold seekers who rushed to California in 1849 (get it—forty-niners?) in hopes of striking it rich in the great California gold rush. After a carpenter found gold near Sutter's Mill in 1848, word spread like wildfire. (Think how mad Mexico was—it had just lost that land!) Gold seekers, mostly men, streamed in from across America and around the world. In the first four years of the gold rush, California's population rose from 20,000 to almost 225,000.

With all those people, there wasn't enough of anything to go around. Prices went sky-high: Flour was $800 a barrel, sugar was $400 a barrel, eggs were $3 apiece, and shovels were $100. (This was at a time when skilled workers made $2 a day.) The backbreaking work of panning for gold actually wasn't the best way to get rich during the gold rush; most of the people who became wealthy made their money from the *miners*, not from the mines. One of these enterprising suppliers was a man who noticed that the miners needed sturdy pants for all their bending, digging, and squatting. The pants he invented to meet their need might be the same kind you're wearing right now: jeans, made by Levi Strauss.

AMERICAN ENGLISH

The gold rush brought new experiences and new words and expressions to American vocabulary. Just a few: *pay dirt, pan out, bonanza, to stake a claim,* and *to strike it rich.*

The gold rush brought many Chinese people across the Pacific Ocean to America because there were wars going on in China and lots of people there were out of work. But life in California, which the Chinese called "Gold Mountain," wasn't much better than it had been in China. Frustrated white men who couldn't find gold looked for someone to blame. They often—unfairly—blamed the Chinese because they looked, spoke, ate, and worshiped differently. Soon the Chinese were forced to make a living doing only certain jobs, like washing clothes or rolling cigars. They were made to live apart from everyone else and to pay extra taxes. They had no rights. Many eventually went home, but those who stayed created "Chinatowns" in the cities where they settled. Today America's two largest Chinatowns are in San Francisco and New York City.

How did the California gold rush heighten the debate over slavery?

So many settlers moved to California so quickly that, by 1849, the territory had enough people (an adult male population of at least sixty thousand) to apply for statehood. The Missouri Compromise only applied to the land gained in the Louisiana Purchase, so again Congress faced the slavery issue. The Oregon Territory was considered free, so southerners wanted California to be a slave state. But California's state constitution forbade slavery.

The Great Compromiser, Henry Clay, now seventy-three years old, again helped keep the Union together. In what became known as the Compromise of 1850, California entered the Union as a free state, but New Mexico and Utah were organized as territories without restrictions on slavery. The compromise also included a Fugitive Slave Law, which made it legal for slave owners to go after and capture any of their slaves who had run away and escaped to the North.

The Fugitive Slave Act was the most controversial part of the compromise. It meant that no black person was safe. Free blacks in the North could be accused of being runaways, captured, and sent south without an opportunity to defend themselves. The act also made it illegal to help or hide escaped slaves. When northerners defied the law, southerners saw that as a violation of their property. The never-ending conflicts over slavery and the two increasingly different ways of life in the North and South made many Americans wonder if the Union could remain together.

Was the Underground Railroad the first subway system?

The Underground Railroad by Charles T. Webber

It sounds like it, but the Underground Railroad was really a network of houses and other safe places for slaves who were running away to freedom in the northern United States or in Canada. It was run by whites and slaves who had already escaped. These people helped the runaways get from one "station" on the railroad to another, usually during the night. The most famous "conductor" of the Railroad was Harriet Tubman (1820?–1913), a slave from Maryland who made her way to freedom in the North in 1849 and immediately returned to the South to help others. She made at least nineteen trips on the Railroad and is said to have been personally responsible for leading more than three hundred slaves to freedom. Not surprisingly, southerners offered rewards as high as $40,000 for her capture. Tubman was never caught. She said, "On my Underground Railroad I never run my train off the track and I have never lost a passenger."

❝ PEOPLE IN GENERAL WILL SAY THEY LIKE COLORED MEN AS WELL AS ANY OTHER, BUT *IN THEIR PROPER PLACE*. THEY ASSIGN US THAT PLACE; THEY DON'T LET US DO IT OURSELVES NOR WILL THEY ALLOW US A VOICE IN THE DECISION. THEY WILL NOT ALLOW THAT WE HAVE A HEAD TO THINK, AND A HEART TO FEEL AND A SOUL TO ASPIRE. . . . THAT'S THE WAY WE ARE LIKED. YOU DEGRADE US, AND THEN ASK WHY WE ARE DEGRADED—YOU SHUT OUR MOUTHS AND THEN ASK WHY WE DON'T SPEAK—YOU CLOSE YOUR COLLEGES AND SEMINARIES AGAINST US, AND THEN ASK WHY WE DON'T KNOW MORE. ❞

—FREDERICK DOUGLASS *(1817–1895), in one of his first recorded antislavery speeches, delivered in Plymouth County, Massachusetts, in 1841*

After Frederick Douglass, a Maryland slave, escaped to the North, he devoted his life to the cause of freedom. He fought for the rights not only of blacks but of women, the poor, Indians, and the Chinese. His powerful, heartfelt speeches made him one of the most famous men in America. During the Civil War, Douglass became an advisor to President Abraham Lincoln and recruited black soldiers to the Union cause. After the war he held many government appointments, including ambassador to Haiti.

When did women write their own Declaration?

When a woman named Elizabeth Cady Stanton (1815–1902) traveled to an antislavery convention in London with her husband in 1840, the women there were made to sit off to the side in a curtained room and were not permitted to speak out. Stanton proposed to another *abolitionist*, or antislavery activist, Lucretia Mott (1793–1880), that they do something about women's rights when they returned home. At this time women were expected to obey their fathers or husbands. Few states gave married women legal right to own property. In no state did they have rights to keep their earnings or their children. The professions that were open to women—almost exclusively writing and schoolteaching—paid them much less than they did men. Women could not be licensed in law or medicine, and only one liberal arts college in the nation admitted females.

In 1848 the Seneca Falls Convention organized by Stanton, Mott, and others became the first public meeting in America devoted to women's rights. About three hundred people, both women and men, met in Seneca Falls, New York, and passed many resolutions, including a demand that women be given the right to vote. In a document called the Declaration of Sentiments, they wrote, "We hold these truths to be self-evident: that all men and women are created equal." They went on to list their grievances, just as Thomas Jefferson had done for the colonists in the Declaration of Independence.

Many newspapers jeered at the women and their reform efforts, but the Seneca Falls Convention prompted conventions in other states and got the women's rights ball rolling. In 1851 Stanton was introduced to another reformer, Susan B. Anthony (1820–1906). They combined their talents and led the movement that would eventually win women the right to vote.

What do a raven, a whale named Moby Dick, and Paul Revere have in common?

They are all characters in early American literature. Before the 1820s, few people read American literature. Why? No one was really writing it. Several generations after the founding of the nation, Americans were beginning to realize they had a common culture and a common past. The United States was growing up. Some of America's first great writers wrote about American life and history. James Fenimore Cooper wrote about the heroic outdoorsman in *The Last of the Mohicans*. Henry Wadsworth Longfellow immortalized the midnight ride of Paul

Revere (see p. 40); Ralph Waldo Emerson described the first shot of the American Revolution as the "shot heard 'round the world." Nathaniel Hawthorne wrote about Puritan New England, and Emerson and Henry David Thoreau about independence and self-reliance. These authors joined other noteworthy early American writers such as Walt Whitman, Herman Melville (who wrote *Moby Dick*), and Edgar Allan Poe (who wrote a famous poem called "The Raven").

But the most influential and widely read book of the nineteenth century was a novel about slavery. Harriet Beecher Stowe's *Uncle Tom's Cabin* (1852) helped many people see that slaves were people, too. In it a religious and virtuous slave named Uncle Tom quietly resists the cruelties of slavery, only to be beaten to death by the plantation overseer. Both black and white characters in the book do good and bad things, implying that a person's character didn't depend on the color of his or her skin. *Uncle Tom's Cabin* illustrated the horrors of slavery in a way no other abolitionist writings did. The novel was banned in much of the South and made northerners even angrier about slavery.

When and where did the slavery debate turn bloody?

In 1854, in Kansas. That year, Illinois Senator Stephen A. Douglas introduced the Kansas-Nebraska Act. The act *repealed*, or undid, the Missouri Compromise and instead said new states would decide for themselves whether to allow slavery. (Under the Missouri Compromise, both Kansas and Nebraska would have been free.)

When the act passed in Congress, both slavery and abolitionist forces streamed into Kansas. Each hoped to outnumber the other and win the territory when it applied for statehood. Fighting soon broke out between the two sides, and within five months some two hundred people had died in "Bloody Kansas." (The antislavery side eventually won; Kansas became a free state.) No one knew it yet, but the fighting was a glimpse of what was to come. Violent civil war would soon take hold of the entire country.

An extreme abolitionist named John Brown (1800–1859) helped set off the bloodshed in Kansas when he led an attack that killed five unarmed proslavery settlers. Brown became obsessed with the idea of freeing slaves by military force, and in 1859 he organized a raid on government weapons stored at Harper's Ferry, Virginia (now West Virginia). Brown planned to seize the weapons and give them to slaves to start a slave revolt. But U.S. army soldiers and marines led by Robert E. Lee (see page 95) surrounded him and his eighteen followers, and ten of his men were killed. Brown was captured, convicted, and hanged six weeks later. He died with unwavering belief that his cause was just. Proslavery forces thought he was a crazed fanatic, but in antislavery camps he became a *martyr*, or saintlike figure.

What was one of the most dreadful decisions the Supreme Court ever made?

It could be the ruling in the 1857 case *Dred Scott* v. *Sandford*. Dred Scott was a slave who had moved with his owner from Missouri to the free territories of Illinois and Wisconsin and back to Missouri. Was he then free, because he had lived in territories where slavery was illegal?

Scott and his lawyers argued that he was. The Supreme Court said he wasn't. In his decision Chief Justice Roger Taney wrote that blacks, free or slave, were not citizens, and that they were "so inferior that they had no rights which a white man was bound to respect," including the right to sue in court. Taney went on to say that Dred Scott was the property of his owner, and since property is protected by the Fifth Amendment to the Constitution, Congress had no right to deprive Scott's owner of his property anywhere in the United States. In Taney's opinion all the compromises that had already restricted slavery were unconstitutional.

Southerners were overjoyed at the decision. Northern abolitionists were enraged. War loomed closer than ever.

CHAPTER 5

The War of Brothers

"'A house divided against itself cannot stand.' I believe this government cannot endure permanently half slave and half free."

—**Abraham Lincoln**, *June 17, 1858*

AMERICAN ★ STORIES

Was Abraham Lincoln (1809–1865) really born in a floorless, one-window log cabin in Kentucky?

Yes. (Though he wasn't the first president to be born in a log cabin. Do you remember who was?) Growing up on the frontiers of Kentucky and Indiana, Lincoln attended only one year of school overall. He taught himself to read and write and devoured every book he could get his hands on. He also loved telling jokes and stories. What he wasn't as fond of was the log splitting, plowing, and building that frontier living demanded, even though his tall, powerful body made him good at such things. So when he was twenty-two, he moved to the town of New Salem, Illinois. There he would get his start in politics, but only after he worked as a country store clerk, a postmaster, and a self-taught lawyer. One day he would be counted among America's greatest presidents.

What were the Lincoln-Douglas debates?

Lincoln lost several elections for the public offices he ran for (though he did manage to get elected to the Illinois legislature, and he also served one term in Congress). His biggest defeat, the loss of the 1858 election for senator from Illinois, set him up for his most important victory.

In 1858 Lincoln was running against Stephen A. Douglas. Since Lincoln was virtually unknown as a candidate, he challenged Douglas to a series of debates around the state. The focus of their talks quickly became slavery. Douglas made Lincoln look like a fierce abolitionist; Lincoln made Douglas appear to be staunchly proslavery. In reality their views weren't much different. Lincoln had never believed in slavery, and though he didn't think he could end it, he knew it was tearing the nation apart.

The Lincoln-Douglas debates attracted huge crowds and made Lincoln famous throughout the country. When Lincoln won the presidency two years later, he beat Douglas by 10 percent of the popular vote, as well as defeating two other candidates in a four-way election.

★ Abraham Lincoln was plainspoken and witty and often made fun of himself. Here are some things he said:

(After some disappointing elections) "[I feel] somewhat like the boy in Kentucky who stubbed his toe while running to see his sweetheart. The boy said he was too big to cry, and far too badly hurt to laugh."

"Nobody has ever expected me to be President. In my poor, lean, lank face nobody has ever seen that any cabbages were sprouting out."

(About newspaper coverage of the Civil War) "I have endured a great deal of ridicule without much malice; and have received a great deal of kindness, not quite free from ridicule. I am used to it."

What did the Southern states think about Lincoln's election as president?

They didn't like it one bit. Many Southerners already felt that they were being pushed around by the North. They also knew that Lincoln, as a Republican, wanted to keep the Union together and end the spread of slavery to new states. So rather than submitting to this "rule," Southern states decided to *secede* from, or leave, the Union.

Within days of Lincoln's election in 1860, South Carolina seceded. Before Lincoln took office, five other states (Alabama, Florida, Georgia, Louisiana, and Mississippi) had followed. Together those six states formed a new government called the Confederate States of America, or the Confederacy. They elected Jefferson Davis, a senator from Mississippi, as their president. Within six months five additional states (Texas, Virginia, Arkansas, North Carolina, and Tennessee) left the Union to join the Confederacy.

★ Not all the slave-holding states seceded from the Union. Kentucky, Missouri, Maryland, and Delaware remained in the Union but continued to keep slaves. These "border states" were joined by West Virginia when it was admitted to the Union in 1863. The new state was formed from the northwestern part of Virginia because the people there opposed slavery and did not wish to secede with the rest of the state. Nevada, in the West, also joined the Union during the Civil War.

MAJOR MILESTONES IN THE AMERICAN CIVIL WAR 1861–1865

1861

APRIL 12   The Civil War begins when Confederates fire on the Union-held Fort Sumter, in the harbor of Charleston, South Carolina. There are no deaths. President Lincoln soon calls for 75,000 volunteers for three months' service in the U.S. army. Most people think the war will be over in a few months.

JULY 21   First Battle of Bull Run, also called First Manassas, in Virginia. Surprised and humiliated by a Confederate victory in this first battle of the war, the Union realizes it had better prepare for a longer war than expected.

1862

MARCH 9   The Union *Monitor* and Confederate *Merrimack*, America's first ironclad ships, fight a key naval battle. Both sides claim victory. The battle begins a new era of warfare, doing away with fragile, flammable wooden ships.

APRIL 6–7   General Ulysses S. Grant wins a hard-fought battle at Shiloh, Tennessee.

SEPTEMBER 17   In Antietam, Maryland, in the bloodiest single day of the war, the dead and wounded top 10,000 on each side.

DECEMBER 13   Despite being greatly outnumbered, General Robert E. Lee's army wins a substantial victory at Fredericksburg, Virginia, lifting the rebels' spirits and confidence. The Union loses 12,000, compared to the Confederates' 5,000.

1863

JANUARY 1   President Lincoln's Emancipation Proclamation takes effect. (See page 98.)

MAY 1–4   Confederates, under Generals Lee and Stonewall Jackson, defeat a larger Union army at Chancellorsville, Virginia. After the battle Jackson is accidentally shot by one of his own men. He dies of pneumonia a week later.

JULY 1–3   In Gettysburg, Pennsylvania, three days of heroic fighting on both sides make for one of the most devastating battles of the war. With the loss of a third of the Confederate army's strength, the Union victory marks a turning point in the war. Combined losses total 51,000 killed, wounded, or missing.

Bodies of soldiers at Gettysburg

JULY 4   The Union wins the siege of Vicksburg, Mississippi, led by General Grant. The Union gains control of the Mississippi River, splitting the Confederacy in two from east to west.

1864

MARCH 10   Grant is named commander of the Union armies.

MAY 3   Grant and the Army of the Potomac enter Virginia to attack Lee and capture Richmond.

SEPTEMBER 2   Union General William T. Sherman occupies Atlanta, Georgia, and sets much of the city on fire.

NOVEMBER 8   Lincoln is reelected president of the United States.

NOVEMBER 15   Sherman begins his infamous March to the Sea, from Atlanta to Savannah, Georgia. He and his men cut a path forty miles wide, again splitting the South in two, this time from north to south. Sherman's army wrecks everything in its way. This "total war" is a new concept, and its brutality devastates the Confederacy.

1865

FEBRUARY 1   Sherman's army starts through the Carolinas on a march as destructive as the March to the Sea.

APRIL 3   Union troops enter Petersburg, Virginia, and the Confederate capital of Richmond.

APRIL 9   General Lee surrenders to General Grant at the village of Appomattox Court House, Virginia.

APRIL 14   President Lincoln is assassinated by John Wilkes Booth at Ford's Theatre in Washington, D.C. He dies the next morning.

MAY 4   The last Confederate army surrenders.

What's so civil about a civil war?

Civil wars get their name because they are conflicts fought among citizens of the same country—not because they are civilized events. In the U.S. Civil War, members of the same family sometimes ending up fighting one another. Even President Lincoln had four brothers-in-law who fought for the Confederacy.

The Civil War was different from earlier American wars in other ways. It saw the first wartime use of the telegraph for communication. For the first time, railroads carried troops and supplies. Ironclad ships were invented and hot-air balloons used for scouting. Mines and hand grenades, along with new kinds of rifles, cannons, and bullets, caused unbelievable, horrible slaughter. In the Civil War men began to dig trenches and foxholes to protect themselves in battle. Rules of war also changed when Union generals began waging all-out war, in which nothing was spared.

About 620,000 people died in the Civil War from battle wounds and disease—far more than in any other war in U.S. history except World War II.

Was the Civil War fought over slavery?

It was, and it wasn't. Most Northerners were not abolitionists, and most Southerners were not slave owners. Slavery was a major issue, but more than that it was the symbol of the economic and lifestyle differences that had long divided the farming South and the industrial North.

In the North industry had become more and more important. Many people worked in cities and factories. While factory workers were usually not rich, they were free. In the South the people who owned slaves held a great deal of power. They were fighting to preserve their wealth, way of life, and what they viewed as their property rights. Slave owners' business was large-scale agriculture, and their profits depended on their unpaid slave labor.

Perhaps most fundamentally, however, Southerners felt they were being pushed around by the North, and they didn't want to be told how to live their lives. Since they believed that states should have more power than the federal government, they said states had a right to leave the Union if they wanted to. So that's exactly what they did. Americans who fought to preserve the Union, of course, didn't agree.

Why didn't the North just let the South go?

Good question. That would have saved a lot of lives. But it also would have meant the end of the United States. If states could just pick up and leave the Union whenever they wanted to, soon there would be just a mess of weak and insignificant "Disunited States." More importantly, the breakup of the Union would have meant the end of the American experiment. To President Lincoln, the war was about holding on to the unique republic the Founders had worked so hard to create. Since the United States was the only significant democratic government in the world, Lincoln believed he was fighting to preserve freedom and democracy around the globe, not just in America.

Did the United States ever have two presidents at once ?

Not exactly—but during the Civil War the Confederacy did not regard Abraham Lincoln as its leader, naming instead Jefferson Davis (1808–1889) as its own president. Davis was born in Kentucky but raised in Mississippi. Wealthy and well educated, he attended West Point and was an officer in the U.S. army for seven years. He later served in the Mexican War, was elected to the U.S. Senate, and became President Franklin Pierce's secretary of war. Davis hoped to command the Confederate army, and was actually disappointed to be named president in 1861. After the war Davis was captured and jailed for two years on charges of treason.

Robert E. Lee

Confederate General Robert E. Lee (1807–1870) came from a famous military family: His father was "Light-Horse Harry" Lee, one of Washington's cavalry heroes from the Revolutionary War. Lee graduated second in his class at West Point and was a hero of the Mexican War. He was nearly ready to retire from military service when the Civil War broke out. President Lincoln offered Lee command of the Union forces, but Lee refused. Even though he was against slavery and secession, he could not bring himself to fight against his family and his home state of Virginia. An expert

Confederate general Robert E. Lee

strategist, Lee was a great leader and the epitome of a general, intelligent and dignified. He was highly respected by both sides. After Lee's death, his estate became a museum and the most famous burial ground in the nation—Arlington National Cemetery.

What was it like to be a soldier in the Civil War?

At the outbreak of the war, soldiers didn't have much training, as both the Union and the Confederacy tried to rush them into battle before the other side could prepare. Many men marched off to war wearing homemade uniforms that might be of any color. (Though when possible, most Union troops wore blue and most Confederates wore gray or *butternut*, a light brownish gray.)

At first so many men volunteered to serve in the armies that neither side knew what to do with them all. But as the conflict wore on, both the Union and Confederacy had to resort to *drafts*, or forcing men to be in the army. Confederates who were drafted but owned twenty or more slaves could be excused from service in the army (though many served anyway). Unionists could pay a substitute to fight for them, which a good number did.

Some men saw going off to war as an adventure. Many had never traveled much beyond their hometowns. But they soon learned that army life was no picnic. Pay was low and rations were scarce, especially in the Confederate army. The usual diet was *hardtack* (hard bread), beans, coffee, rice, and bacon. Both sides resorted to hunting, gathering nuts and berries, and stealing livestock and food from farmers. Troops often slept on the ground while at a battle and in makeshift cabins in between. In their downtime soldiers enjoyed storytelling by the campfire, playing checkers and horseshoes, writing letters, singing, and holding races and other contests.

Sickness was common in army camps, and especially in military prisons. Twice as many soldiers died of sickness as died in battle. Medical supplies were short, and doctors, including surgeons, had little training. Hospitals were often tents strung out in the open if an abandoned building couldn't be found. *Antisepsis*—the practice of cleaning germs from surgical tools and coverings—had not taken hold in American medicine at the time of the war. Conditions were so unsanitary that many soldiers died of infection. Surgeons cut off limbs with saws and kept patients quiet with doses of whiskey or brandy to dull the shock and pain. One observer described a doctor's technique following the battle of Gettsyburg: "The surgeon snatched his knife from between his teeth, where it had been while his hands were busy, wiped it rapidly once or twice across his blood-stained apron, and the cutting began."

⭐ Just like in the Revolutionary War (and any war), supporters working at home were busy. Women made uniforms and rolled bandages, worked in factories making shells and in hospitals nursing the wounded, and sponsored more than twenty thousand relief organizations. Girls helped their mothers while boys took over the chores their soldiering fathers had done. Those at home suffered some of the same hardships as the soldiers. Food was so scarce, especially in the South, that many civilians starved to death.

Who served in the armies?

Mostly white men, but they were not alone in battle. About three hundred women enlisted in the armies disguised as male soldiers, and an unknown number worked as spies. About three thousand women also served as nurses, a profession that had been almost exclusively male until the war.

Children as young as eight or nine joined the armies as drummer boys. Many Civil War soldiers were not much older. Some estimates say that 10 to 20 percent of soldiers were under the age of eighteen. There was no way for recruiters to prove a person's age, and the armies, especially in the Confederacy, needed everyone they could get. Some boys wrote the number 18 on a piece of paper and put it in their shoe so they could tell the recruiter they were "over 18."

Blacks also helped fill the ranks. In the Confederate army they didn't serve as soldiers but as servants for their masters who did. Slaves cooked, washed uniforms, dug trenches, built fortifications, and did other unpopular jobs. In the Union army the first free blacks and runaway slaves to enlist were allowed to serve only as cooks and scouts. But that changed after the Emancipation Proclamation became effective on January 1, 1863. Then, more than two hundred thousand blacks enlisted in the Union army and navy. Blacks were paid less than whites and given the worst jobs, but when they had a chance to fight, they gained respect and changed Northerners' views about blacks as soldiers. The 54th

AMERICAN ENGLISH

The Civil War gave the country some new sayings, as well as some new practices. Americans say:

—skedaddle, which became popular when Union troops used it to describe Confederate forces fleeing from battle

—the grapevine, meaning (usually unreliable) rumors

—AWOL for *absent without leave* (from the army)

—pup tents, for small, two-man shelters

—sideburns, after the muttonchop facial hair worn by Union Commander Ambrose Burnside

Massachusetts, the first black regiment recruited in the North, led an attack on Fort Wagner, South Carolina, in 1863, fighting well and bravely. (The regiment's heroism was captured in the 1989 movie *Glory*.) After that several black regiments played significant roles in a number of major battles. Twenty-three blacks from the army and navy eventually received the Congressional Medal of Honor, the highest military award in America.

⭐ One of the most famous youths of the war was Johnny Clem, who ran away to join the Union army in 1861, when he was only nine. He tagged along with the 22nd Massachusetts until that regiment adopted him as their drummer boy. In 1863 he was allowed to enlist in the army. At the age of eleven he shot a Confederate officer who tried to take him prisoner, then played dead until he could escape. Young John was promoted to lance corporal. After the war he reenlisted in the army and became a career general.

SETTING IT STRAIGHT

Did the Emancipation Proclamation free the slaves?

No, and yes. A proclamation is an official public statement, not a law. Nevertheless, the government could enforce the Emancipation Proclamation because of the powers given to Lincoln as commander in chief in a time of war. The proclamation didn't free slaves in the border states, because those states were not at war with the U.S. Slaves in border states could only be freed by a constitutional amendment or by the state lawmakers. The Emancipation Proclamation freed slaves only in rebel territory, small parts of which were controlled by Union troops. But the basic idea of the proclamation was to state that if the Union won the war, slavery would be over. Lincoln had come to realize that he could not save the Union as a democracy without abolishing slavery. He announced the Emancipation Proclamation in September 1862, and it took effect on January 1, 1863.

The Emancipation Proclamation changed the focus of the war. In some ways, it made the war less popular in the North. Soldiers who had been willing to fight for preservation of the Union were less eager to fight for slaves they feared would come and take their jobs. But the proclamation was well received in Europe, where it prevented England and France from recognizing the independence of the South. More importantly, it also gave hope to the nearly 4 million slaves who still lived in bondage.

> ⭐ A West Point graduate, George McClellan (1826–1885) became general-in-chief of the Union armies in 1861 and was a great organizer who inspired his men. He had *almost* all the qualities of a great general. The problem was that he hated to fight. He hung back, made excuses, and dawdled. It got so bad that Lincoln once said, "If McClellan is not using the army, I should like to borrow it for a while." McClellan was replaced as general-in-chief in 1862.

What did Lincoln do in three minutes?

On November 19, 1863, a ceremony was held to dedicate the national cemetery at Gettysburg, Pennsylvania. Edward Everett, a statesman and one of the greatest speakers of the day, delivered a two-and-a-half-hour speech. President Lincoln spoke for less than three minutes. Yet the president's words gave a clear, thoughtful, even poetic statement of what the war was all about. Today the Gettysburg Address is probably the most famous speech ever given by a president.

> ⭐ Lincoln did not write the Gettysburg Address on the back of an envelope while on the train to Gettysburg, as legend has it. He wrote most of it before he got to Pennsylvania and finished it the night before he spoke.

"Four score and seven years ago our fathers brought forth on this continent, a new nation, conceived in Liberty, and dedicated to the proposition that all men are created equal.

"Now we are engaged in a great civil war, testing whether that nation, or any nation so conceived and so dedicated, can long endure. We are met on a great battlefield of that war. We have come to dedicate a portion of that field as a final resting place for those who here gave their lives that the nation might live. It is altogether fitting and proper that we should do this.

"But, in a larger sense, we can not dedicate—we can not consecrate—we can not hallow this ground. The brave men, living and dead, who struggled here, have consecrated it far above our poor power to add or detract. The world will little note, nor long remember what we say here, but it can never forget what they did here. It is for us the living, rather, to be dedicated here to the unfinished work which they who fought here have thus far so nobly advanced. It is rather for us to be here dedicated to the great task remaining before us—that from these honored dead we take increased devotion to that cause for which they gave the last full measure of devotion—that we here highly resolve that these dead shall not have died in vain—that this nation, under God, shall have a new birth of freedom—and that government of the people, by the people, for the people, shall not perish from the earth."

—President Abraham Lincoln, *the Gettysburg Address*

Whose nickname was "Unconditional Surrender"?

U. S. Grant (1822–1885), the sixth and final commander of the Union forces. Ulysses S. Grant was born Hiram Ulysses Grant, but when he was registered at West Point as Ulysses Simpson Grant, he didn't correct the mistake. From his days as a shy child in Ohio, Grant loved horses and was an excellent rider. He hoped to be assigned to the cavalry (the division of the army that fought mainly on horseback) upon graduation from West Point, but since there were no openings at the time, he was placed in the infantry (the division that fought mostly on foot). Grant fought in the Mexican War and remained in the army until 1854. He

Union general U. S. Grant

failed at several jobs before returning to the military when the Civil War broke out. Though he was not a model soldier, he was a determined and brilliant fighter. As the sixth general to head the Union forces, he was finally what Lincoln had been searching for. His strategy of finding the enemy and hitting them with everything he had cost many lives on both sides, but eventually brought an end to the war. He later served two terms as president of the United States. His memoirs, which he finished days before he died in 1885, were an instant best-seller.

Why was the surrender as important as the victory in the Civil War?

Because the terms of surrender would determine how—or rather if—the nation would come back together. President Lincoln worried that when it came time for the Confederate armies to surrender, small groups of resisters might hold out in the South for years to come. That would make rebuilding the nation very difficult, if not impossible. Lincoln's plan for *Reconstruction*, or the rebuilding and reunification of the United States, called for binding up the nation's wounds "with malice toward none, with charity for all." He would welcome the rebel states back into the Union as long as they pledged to uphold the Constitution (which included the Thirteenth Amendment, abolishing slavery) and the Emancipation Proclamation. Lincoln felt that if the rebels were treated well they would return their loyalty to the Union more easily and the nation could move forward.

When the surrender came on April 9, 1865, the generals on both sides rose to the occasion. Though General Lee said he would rather die a thousand deaths than surrender to General Grant, he held his head high and met the fate of his army with dignity. Grant offered generous terms of peace and made sure the Confederates, though defeated, were not robbed of their self-respect.

After the surrender Lee told his men to lay down their weapons. "Go home now," he said, "and if you make as good citizens as you have soldiers, you will do well, and I shall always be proud of you."

AMERICAN VOICES

❝WHAT GENERAL LEE'S FEELINGS WERE I DO NOT KNOW. AS HE WAS A MAN OF MUCH DIGNITY, WITH AN IMPASSIBLE FACE . . . HIS FEELINGS . . . WERE ENTIRELY CONCEALED FROM MY OBSERVATION; BUT MY OWN FEELINGS . . . WERE SAD AND DEPRESSED. I FELT LIKE ANYTHING RATHER THAN REJOICING AT THE DOWNFALL OF A FOE WHO HAD FOUGHT SO LONG AND VALIANTLY AND HAD SUFFERED SO MUCH FOR A CAUSE, THOUGH THAT CAUSE WAS, I BELIEVE, ONE OF THE WORST FOR WHICH PEOPLE EVER FOUGHT. . . .

"GENERAL LEE WAS DRESSED IN A FULL UNIFORM WHICH WAS ENTIRELY NEW, AND WAS WEARING A SWORD OF CONSIDERABLE VALUE. . . . IN MY ROUGH TRAVELING SUIT . . . I MUST HAVE

CONTRASTED VERY STRANGELY WITH A MAN SO HANDSOMELY
DRESSED, SIX FEET HIGH AND OF FAULTLESS FORM. . . .

"WE SOON FELL INTO A CONVERSATION ABOUT OLD ARMY TIMES. . . .
OUR CONVERSATION GREW SO PLEASANT THAT I ALMOST FORGOT
THE OBJECT OF OUR MEETING. **"**

—GENERAL ULYSSES S. GRANT, *remembering the surrender at*
Appomattox Court House

In many ways the Civil War gave the United States what President
Lincoln had hoped for in the Gettysburg Address—"a new birth of
freedom." Some historians say that the end of the Civil War was actually
the true birth of the nation. What had been a collection of loosely bound
individual states and an experiment in republican government emerged
from the bloodshed a unified country that was more clearly devoted to
the freedoms put forth during the American Revolution. The Civil War
strengthened the nation, the federal government, and the rights
guaranteed by the Constitution.

Why didn't Reconstruction go as President Lincoln had planned?

Because he wasn't around to see it through. On April 14, 1865,
just five days after Lee's surrender, President Lincoln was shot
in the back of the head while watching a play at Ford's Theatre
in Washington, D.C. He was taken to a house across the street
and attended by doctors, but there was nothing they could do.
The president died the next morning, the first president in
American history to be assassinated. The nation went into
mourning, dazed and deeply saddened.

The assassin was a twenty-seven-year-old actor named John
Wilkes Booth, who came from the border state of Maryland but
was an ardent supporter of the Confederacy. He and his fellow
conspirators tried to kill not only President Lincoln but also
Vice President Andrew Johnson and Secretary of State William
Seward the same night; Johnson's would-be assassin chickened
out at the last minute, and Seward was attacked but survived.
Booth's goal was to avenge the South, but in killing Lincoln he

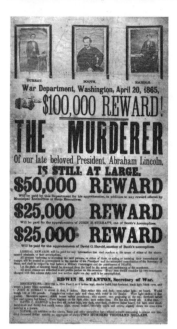

War Department, Washington, April 20, 1865,

$100,000 REWARD!

THE MURDERER

Of our late beloved President, Abraham Lincoln,

IS STILL AT LARGE.

$50,000 REWARD

$25,000 REWARD

$25,000 REWARD

EDWIN M. STANTON, Secretary of War.

Booth and his two conspirators were wanted for murder.

hurt the South most of all. Southerners had had a friend in Lincoln and his compassionate policies. Sadly much of his vision for Reconstruction died with him.

What was reconstructed during Reconstruction?

Reconstruction was a busy, chaotic time full of difficult, important questions and bitter power struggles between Republicans (who were mostly Northerners and Southern blacks) and Democrats (who were mostly white Southerners). Without Lincoln's strength and foresight, many unfortunate things happened that hurt and divided the nation all over again.

Vice President Andrew Johnson became President Johnson when Lincoln was killed. So it was he who faced the enormous questions of Reconstruction: how to rebuild a South that was in shambles; what to do with nearly 4 million newly freed slaves; how to reconstruct Southern governments and readmit states to the Union; and how, if at all, to punish the former Confederate leaders.

⭐ During Lincoln's presidency, Congress established the Freedmen's Bureau to help former slaves make the transition to freedom. The bureau built hospitals and provided medical care, created more than four thousand free schools from elementary grades through college for black young people, and gave out food and clothing to blacks and whites alike.

What were "Black Codes"?

They were bad news. The former rebel states were readmitted to the Union after they had ratified the Thirteenth Amendment to the Constitution, which abolished slavery. Once readmitted, the Southern states elected former Confederate leaders and army officers to Congress and passed laws called "Black Codes" that got around the Thirteenth Amendment by denying blacks their rights. Republicans were outraged. A group of Republicans known as Radicals passed a Civil Rights Act in 1866 to override the Black Codes. President Johnson, a Southern Democrat (Lincoln, himself a Republican, had chosen Johnson as a running mate to win votes in the border states), vetoed the act, but the Republicans in Congress had enough votes to override the veto, for the first time in American history.

The override of the veto showed that the Republican majority in Congress clearly had more power than the president. Congress took over Reconstruction and divided the South into military regions. It sent in soldiers to make sure blacks were treated fairly and to register them to vote. Congress then required states to rewrite their state constitutions to allow blacks to vote and to ratify the Fourteenth Amendment, which made all former slaves citizens and said states could not deny any person his or her constitutional rights. With the addition of the Fifteenth Amendment in 1869, black males (but still not American Indians or women) gained the right to vote for president and members of Congress.

What did Congress almost do to President Johnson?

a) hide his lunch money

b) kick him out of office

c) rearrange all the furniture at the White House

The answer is letter *b*. Andrew Johnson was the first president in American history to be *impeached*, or accused of crime while in office. Impeachment means the president will be removed from office if found guilty. (Basically, he will be fired.)

President Johnson was accused of violating the Tenure of Office Act, which said that the president couldn't remove any government official without the consent of Congress. The act had just been passed by Congress in 1867 and was designed to keep allies of the Radical Republicans in office. President Johnson said it was unconstitutional for Congress to pass such an act. To test it, he removed Secretary of War Edwin Stanton from office. Johnson was promptly impeached by the House of Representatives.

Johnson had to stand trial before the Senate. By just one vote, the Senate found him not guilty of the "high crimes and misdemeanors" necessary to remove a president from office. (No hard feelings, though—he served out his term and years later he became the only former president elected to the Senate.)

Did any blacks get involved in politics during Reconstruction?

Between 1869 and 1876, seventeen black men were elected to Congress. More than six hundred blacks also served in their state legislatures, and hundreds more held other local offices. Many of these men had been free before the war and had even gone to college in the North. But others were former slaves, recruited by Republicans to run for office. Republicans supported black voting and officeholding because they knew blacks would vote for their party—the party of Lincoln, who had freed them. The Republicans wanted to keep the power they had had during the war, when Democrats were mostly absent.

How did Reconstruction end?

With a close presidential election. After the election in 1876, Democrats said that their candidate, Samuel Tilden, had won. Republicans said Democrats had intimidated voters in some states, and they withheld those states' electoral votes. After months of bickering over the election results, political leaders reached a compromise. Democrats would accept Republican candidate Rutherford B. Hayes as president if all federal troops would be removed from the South. Hayes agreed. Reconstruction was over.

By 1877 the troops were gone and whites regained control over state governments. Without the troops and government to protect them, blacks lost nearly everything they'd gained. Planters cheated freedmen and Southern governments passed laws that kept poor blacks working on the planters' land. Other new laws made it virtually impossible for blacks to vote and segregated blacks from whites in schools, libraries, hotels, rest rooms, trains, parks, hospitals, restaurants, and other places. The laws that legalized segregation were called "Jim Crow" laws. They were named after a fictitious character in the song "Jim Crow," written by a white man named Thomas Dartmouth "Daddy" Rice. In the song, Jim Crow sang and danced and didn't give anyone any trouble. There wasn't a lot blacks could do about Jim Crow's racism and discrimination, since they couldn't vote. And unfortunately, Jim Crow was going to be around for a long time.

⭐ After Reconstruction hundreds of thousands of Southern blacks moved north and west in hopes of being treated more fairly than they had been in the South. The biggest migration of blacks took place between 1878 and 1880, when thousands who called themselves Exodusters moved to Kansas, Oklahoma, Iowa, and Nebraska.

GREAT AMERICAN PASTIMES

What sport became more popular after the Civil War?

Think peanuts and Cracker Jacks and the seventh-inning stretch. It's baseball! Though the game, called by the name "rounders," had been played for some time in England and America, the rules were actually written down by an amateur team named the New York Knickerbockers in 1845. The sport grew in popularity and more teams were organized in the Northeast until they were interrupted by the Civil War. Union soldiers brought interest in the sport to other parts of the country, and

after the war more people played baseball than ever before. In 1869 the Cincinnati Red Stockings became America's first professional baseball team.

CHAPTER 6

How the West Was Won . . .
and Lost

"Give me your tired, your poor,
Your huddled masses yearning to breathe free,
The wretched refuse of your teeming shore.
Send these, the homeless, tempest-tost to me,
I lift my lamp beside the golden door!"

—EMMA LAZARUS, *"The New Colossus," 1883*

Who taught a group of Indians on the Great Plains to speak German?

All the Germans who had settled near them. Before the Civil War, millions of immigrants had come to America not only from Germany but from England, Ireland, and the countries of Scandinavia, along with smaller numbers from China, Poland, Russia, and other places. Some immigrants came because they were persecuted in their own countries. Others were poor and wanted a fresh start in America's spacious West. Between 1847 and 1854, a quarter of the entire Irish population, 1.6 million immigrants, came from that country alone. A disease had ruined the potato crops in Ireland, leaving its poorer people starving and desperate.

At first most immigrants settled in northern cities. But when the urban areas became increasingly crowded, many pushed west. Some Americans went west to avoid the Civil War or to start over once the fighting ended. As the far West—Oregon, Washington, California, Utah—filled up, settlers began to carve out homes on the Great Plains. The plains had been passed over at first because the area was Indian Territory, and the dry, barren land looked unfit for farming. But the American population grew and people began to think again about the plains. The government pushed the Indians onto smaller and smaller reservations, and the Homestead Act was signed in 1862. The act gave 160 acres of land to anyone who paid a ten-dollar filing fee and agreed to improve the land for five years.

So many immigrants poured into the United States during the 1860s that, despite the 620,000 deaths in the Civil War, the nation had more people after the war than before it.

If you lived on the plains, what challenges might you encounter?

a) blizzards and frigid winters

b) flooding and tornadoes

c) drought, dust storms, and prairie fires

d) grasshoppers devouring crops

e) loneliness

f) plowing the hard, dry prairie land

Chances are, you might face them all. Winter on the plains often meant bitter cold and blinding blizzards that could kill anyone who was caught outside for too long. The spring brought tornadoes and floods, which gave way to hailstorms and drought in the summer.

The hot, dry weather stirred up dust storms and made conditions perfect for prairie fires. Some years grasshoppers came and ate nearly everything in sight, ruining crops in a matter of hours and eating leather, cloth, curtains, fence posts, door frames, and food in cupboards. Year-round there was loneliness, as neighbors could be a mile or two but sometimes as many as thirty miles away. The whole world seemed to be an endless expanse of sky and grass. And although the soil under that grass was very fertile, it was so firm that farmers could hardly cut through it to plow their fields. (It was so dense that they cut it into bricks and built houses called "soddies.")

The loneliness would ease as more settlers arrived and railroads were built, and new inventions would make farming easier. Windmills pumped water out of underground wells, barbed wire kept cattle from wandering into planted fields, and John Deere's steel plow sliced through the hard soil in a way the old wooden and iron plows never could. But the Industrial Revolution really came to the prairie with Cyrus McCormick's mechanical reaper, which cut and harvested wheat so that farmers didn't have to do the backbreaking work by hand. The reaper made large farms practical and, along with railroads that could carry their crops across the country, changed the way Midwesterners farmed. In turn they changed the environment of the very land they settled.

AMERICAN VOICES

66 THE WIND WHISTLED THROUGH THE WALLS IN WINTER AND THE DUST BLEW IN SUMMER, BUT WE PAPERED THE WALLS WITH NEWSPAPERS AND MADE RAG CARPETS FOR THE FLOOR, AND THOUGHT WE WERE LIVING WELL, VERY ENTHUSIASTIC OVER THE NEW COUNTRY WE INTENDED TO CONQUER. 99

—*Kansas homesteader* LYDIA LYON, *describing her family's new home*

Many historians believe that the taming of the frontier, with its opportunities and freedoms, was what made America the unique place it is today. Those who went west were tough, determined, and brave. The journey westward and the task of carving a new life out of the wilderness were not easy, and doing these things inspired resourcefulness in many a pioneer.

One area in which freedom and independence influenced thinking in the West was women's rights. In Wyoming women won the right to vote and hold state office in 1869 (and in Colorado, Idaho, and Utah by 1900)—decades before the Nineteenth Amendment to the Constitution gave all American women the right to vote in 1920.

Were there any other frontiers?

Yes, Alaska. Although Secretary of State William H. Seward bought Alaska from Russia for only about two cents an acre in 1867, people still questioned the value of the purchase. Most Americans thought the land was worthless and called it "Seward's Icebox" and "Seward's Folly." But that opinion changed in 1896, when gold was found in Alaska's Klondike region. Suddenly Seward had made a great real-estate deal!

Of course, the new land held more than gold—it was home to many distinct Native cultures, including those of the Aleuts, Athabascans, and Tlingit. Ignored or abused by the newcomers to their country, many Native Alaskans later died in the great flu epidemic of 1918.

 The best job in the West was being a cowboy.

False. Cowboys are one of America's most celebrated symbols of bravery, individualism, courage, honor, and fearless independence. After all, cowboys spent their days taming bucking broncos. Didn't they?

Actually, cowboys spent at least fourteen hours a day in their saddles, poking, prodding, and guiding longhorn cattle from Texas to railway towns on the plains, where the animals would

Spanish-speaking cowboys brought many new words into the American language. Among them were *rodeo, stampede, lasso, ranch,* and *bronco.*

be shipped to eastern cities. Cowboys' work was dirty, dangerous, and often dull. A cattle drive took two to three months, during which time cowboys rode among rattlesnakes, insects, and hostile Indian tribes, and in sun, rain, wind, sleet, hail, and even snow. The combination of low pay and long days meant that only one out of three cowboys returned for more than one drive. Their skills did come into play when the cattle got scared and stampeded wildly across the prairie—that's when the cowboys had to use their lassos. If a cowboy made one wrong move in that mass of horns and hooves, he'd likely lose his life.

But the rest of the cowboy image is generally a lot of hogwash made up by journalists and trashy novelists of the time (and movie and television producers of more recent times). In reality, many cowboys were the poorest of the poor, loners and misfits who couldn't get jobs elsewhere or those who had lost their families, friends, and land in the Civil War. Most were young and had little education. They came from many places—the South, the East, the Midwest, and even as far away as Europe. About one in six was Mexican, and about the same number were black. Some were full- or half-blood Indians, and some weren't cowboys at all—they were cowgirls.

The heyday of the cowboy lasted from about 1867 to 1887. The invention of barbed wire in

1873 meant the closing of the open range, as farmers fenced off their land to keep cattle out. When "wars" broke out between cattlemen and farmers, the farmers won. When new railroad lines and refrigerated cars came to the cows, instead of the other way around, the cowboy's fate was sealed.

GREAT AMERICAN PASTIMES
What did pioneers think could "bee" fun ways to work?

Pioneers had so much to do that even their playtime was useful. Families came together to help raise one another's barns and cabins and to cooperate at quilting and other "bees," or work parties. At these parties they would tackle big jobs like husking corn, preserving food, or making soap or candles. When the day's chores were done, they celebrated with a feast, music, and dancing.

Every so often pioneer families escaped work altogether to enjoy county fairs, weddings, picnics, and contests of every sort—from pie eating to shooting, weight lifting, and trying to catch a greased pig!

How did "Buffalo Bill" Cody get his nickname?

From all the buffalo he killed to feed the workers who were building the transcontinental railroad. As the railroad began to cut the Great Plains in half in the 1860s, the West became less of a place where the buffalo could roam—and less of a place where buffalo-dependent Indians could support themselves. The Indians fought the coming of the train, sometimes attacking railroad workers, raiding their supplies, or pulling up freshly laid track. But outnumbered and overpowered, there was little the Indians could do.

People began to talk of a coast-to-coast railroad in the 1850s. As the West opened up, farmers needed fast, cheap transportation to send cattle and wheat back east. In 1862 the Pacific Railroad Act was signed. It called for building a railroad from Omaha, Nebraska (where the eastern railroad lines left off), to Sacramento, California. Work began the following year.

Two companies were building the railroad. The Central Pacific started from California and built east, while the Union Pacific started from Nebraska and built west. The project was a sort of race, because whichever company laid more track got more money and more land beside the rail lines from the government.

Building a railroad across North America was backbreaking work, especially without the heavy machines workers have today. Materials had to be brought in from long distances. Then workers had to lay every four-hundred-pound rail by hand and hammer each spike into place. Engineers had to build bridges over rivers and valleys. Thousands and thousands of men worked to build the railroad. The Union Pacific employed many former Civil War soldiers, blacks, and Irish immigrants. The Central Pacific, short on labor, recruited many Chinese immigrants. The Chinese were often given the most dangerous tasks—like lighting explosives to blast through mountains. Though they became experts at their jobs, thousands died along the way.

GREAT AMERICAN PASTIMES

What should you do if you can't go to the circus?

Let the circus come to you! After 1869 traveling circuses, complete with wild animals, bands, clowns, and high-wire acts, became a popular form of entertainment throughout the West. The biggest and best was P. T. Barnum's "Greatest Show on Earth," which toured the country wowing audiences with elephants, lions, tigers, camels, and nearly four hundred human performers.

The spectacle that probably did more than anything else to fix the romanticized image of the West in people's eyes was Buffalo Bill's Wild West Show. The show, which began in Nebraska in 1881, included daredevil cowboy feats, sharpshooting by the famous Annie Oakley, re-creations of battles between Indians and the army, and Wild West shootouts. Buffalo Bill's show played not only in the West, but all over the United States and even in Europe, giving people who had never been to the West a false impression of what the American frontier was all about.

How did the transcontinental railroad change America?

When the Union Pacific and Central Pacific met at Promontory Summit, Utah, in 1869, their amazing feat of engineering changed the face of the nation. It cleared the land of buffalo and pushed Indians onto

Engineers shake hands at Promontory Summit.

reservations. New railway towns were born. For the first time ever, there were time zones and synchronized clocks to coordinate trains between those towns. Trains brought thousands of new pioneers to the plains, as a five-month journey became one of just eight days. Now America was united in a whole new way, as news, crops, people, and goods could travel between East and West as never before.

Was the settling of the American West a heroic achievement?

To the pioneers it was. But to the Indians, it was another chapter in the ongoing battle for their homelands. The endless stream of white settlers forced the Plains Indians, and the many other tribes who had been removed

★ A full quarter of the army's troops in the West were black soldiers. They were called Buffalo Soldiers by the Indians, who thought the soldiers' hair looked like the hair of the buffalo. Since the Indians honored the buffalo as a sacred animal, the soldiers were honored to be given the name and adopted the buffalo as their emblem.

to the plains, onto smaller and smaller reservations. Though the government had signed treaties granting tribes large blocks of land where no one else could settle, these promises were ignored until every treaty—some four hundred in all in American history—had been broken.

Many tribes would not give up their land and way of life quietly. Between 1865 and 1890, Indians and the U.S. army fought more than two hundred battles. Together these battles are called the Plains Indian Wars.

Who was left standing at Custer's Last Stand?

Sioux and Cheyenne warriors, led by Sioux chiefs Crazy Horse and Sitting Bull. Custer's Last Stand, also known as the Battle of the Little Bighorn, took place in the Montana Territory in 1876. It was the Indians' last and largest victory during the Plains Indian Wars.

Custer's Last Stand was largely the result of one very big ego— that of U.S. Lieutenant Colonel George Armstrong Custer. Custer was ordered to observe a large Sioux camp. He decided to attack, paying no attention to warnings that his army would be greatly outnumbered. "There are not Indians enough in the country to whip the 7th Cavalry," Custer boasted. Yet his 225 men were approaching 2,500 Sioux. Within just one hour, Custer and all the men with him were dead. Custer's defeat embarrassed and angered the American government, causing it to fight even more aggressively against the Indians. Many historians say that the anger created by Custer's Last Stand led to the slaughter of Sioux men, women, and children at Wounded Knee, ending the Indian wars in 1890.

AMERICAN VOICES

❝WE PREFERRED OUR OWN WAY OF LIVING. WE WERE NO EXPENSE TO THE GOVERNMENT. ALL WE WANTED WAS PEACE AND TO BE LEFT ALONE. SOLDIERS WERE SENT OUT IN THE WINTER, WHO DESTROYED OUR VILLAGES.

"THEN 'LONG HAIR' [CUSTER] CAME IN THE SAME WAY. THEY SAY WE MASSACRED HIM, BUT HE WOULD HAVE DONE THE SAME THING TO US HAD WE NOT DEFENDED OURSELVES AND FOUGHT TO THE LAST.❞

—From the last words of CRAZY HORSE, who was killed after surrendering in 1877

Was it only Plains Indians who were forced onto reservations around this time?

Unfortunately, no. Indians throughout the West were meeting the same fate. Some fought fiercely for their land. The famous Apache warrior Geronimo led so many successful attacks against the army that at one point the U.S. government considered him its chief enemy and offered a $25,000 reward for his capture. By 1877 the Apache had been forced onto reservations. But in 1882 and again in 1885, Geronimo planned escapes and led resistance efforts from mountain camps in Mexico. After more than thirty years of fighting, Geronimo surrendered in 1886 and lived the rest of his life in army forts in Florida, Alabama, and Oklahoma.

Chief Joseph of the Nez Percé, who lived near the border of present-day Oregon and Washington, resisted in a different way. The Nez Percé were not hostile people; they had befriended trappers, traders, and explorers since the days of Lewis and Clark. Chief Joseph did not want to fight, but he also refused to sign treaties giving up his homeland. Yet in 1877 fighting did break out when an angry young Nez Percé killed some white

Peaceful Nez Percé warrior Chief Joseph

men. Rather than surrendering to life on a reservation, Joseph led his people on a flight to Canada. Soldiers chased them along the thousand-mile journey. Finally the Nez Percé were surrounded, just forty miles from Canada and freedom. When Chief Joseph died at a reservation in Washington State in 1904, the doctor listed the cause of death as a broken heart.

❝OUR CHIEFS ARE KILLED. . . . THE OLD MEN ARE ALL DEAD. . . . THE LITTLE CHILDREN ARE FREEZING TO DEATH. MY PEOPLE, SOME OF THEM HAVE RUN AWAY TO THE HILLS AND HAVE NO BLANKETS, NO FOOD. NO ONE KNOWS WHERE THEY ARE, PERHAPS FREEZING TO DEATH. I WANT TO HAVE TIME TO LOOK FOR MY CHILDREN AND SEE HOW MANY OF THEM I CAN FIND. MAYBE I CAN FIND THEM AMONG THE DEAD. HEAR ME, MY CHIEFS. MY HEART IS SICK AND SAD. FROM WHERE THE SUN NOW STANDS I WILL FIGHT NO MORE FOREVER.**❞**

—CHIEF JOSEPH, *to the Nez Percé tribe, October 1877*

Who were the robber barons, and whom did they rob?

While the U.S. government was robbing the Indians of their land, big businessmen known as robber barons were "robbing" a good portion of the American people.

In feudal times in Europe, some wealthy landowners would steal from travelers who passed through their lands. These not-so-noble noblemen became known as "robber barons." (*Baron* is a nobleman's title, like *lord* or *earl*.) After the Civil War in America, different kinds of robber barons came along. They didn't steal directly from travelers passing through their lands, but they found other unethical and even illegal ways to build enormous fortunes. They became so rich and powerful that people began to call them robber barons too. The secret of their wealth lay in the big businesses they built—and the way they built them.

Thanks to new machines, America's rich natural resources, and plenty of cheap labor, big industries continued to boom after the Civil War. Some of the men who controlled these industries had made fortunes during the war by making weapons, uniforms, and food for soldiers. Most of them hadn't fought themselves because they could pay for substitutes to take their places, which was allowed.

They added to their wartime fortunes by building railroads, mills, shipyards, oil wells, and factories. Soon some of these men controlled whole industries.

Using unethical means, like manipulating stock and unfair labor practices, they drove rivals out of business until all competition was gone. This created *monopolies*, but it isn't a game.

When people control all of the supplies, they can set prices as high as they want. Think about it. If you have the only lemonade stand on the block, you have a monopoly and can charge whatever people can afford or will agree to pay. But if somebody opens a lemonade stand down the street and charges less, you either have to lower your price or lose the business. That is the competition that is at the heart of a free market. But the robber barons owned all the lemonade stands—along with the lemons, the sugar, the water, and the glasses.

The American robber barons could get away with running roughshod over their consumers and employees because this kind of large-scale industry was new to America and there were few laws to control them. Many government officials simply went along because they believed that such businesses were good for America. Others were dishonest and took bribes. A few large companies were becoming larger and richer. At the same time, many average working people were stuck in terrible poverty. For better or worse, America was becoming the world's wealthiest industrial nation. A relatively weak country at the end of the Civil War, the United States had become, by 1915, the largest producer of food, coal, iron, and steel in the world.

The Biggest of the Big Businessmen

- Cornelius Vanderbilt (1794–1877) first built a steamship empire, then the largest single railroad line in America, the New York Central. When he died, he left most of his fortune to his family, who built a seventy-room mansion in Newport, Rhode Island. The family once threw a party where guests dug in sandboxes filled with diamonds and other precious gems.

- Andrew Carnegie (1835–1919) revolutionized the steel industry with a new, efficient method of turning iron to steel. (Steel is a stronger, more flexible, and lighter form of iron, and it became the foundation of the nation's industrial growth.) Carnegie had come to America with his poor Scottish parents and started working when he was twelve, and his was truly a rags-to-riches story. After another rich businessman, J. P. Morgan, bought Carnegie's company, Carnegie gave away most of his fortune— $324,657,399 in all—to schools, artists, and foundations. He built nearly three thousand public libraries and Carnegie Hall in New York City.

- John D. Rockefeller (1839–1937) founded the Standard Oil Company in 1870. Soon the company owned more than 90 percent of America's oil refineries. Rockefeller kept his costs low by buying up companies that let him pump, refine, and sell his oil himself. He also made secret deals with railroads to get low rates for shipping. Later in life Rockefeller gave away half his fortune—more than $500,000,000—to start the University of Chicago, the Rockefeller Institute for Medical Research, and a charitable foundation.

- John Pierpont Morgan (1837–1913) and his bank, J. P. Morgan and Company, controlled American shipping, telephones, telegraphs, electric power, insurance, and, by 1900, half the nation's railroad tracks. After he bought Carnegie's steel company, Morgan bought huge amounts of iron ore from Rockefeller and founded U.S. Steel Corporation, the nation's first billion-dollar corporation. Morgan was so wealthy and powerful that in 1907 he was able to arrange loans that bailed the U.S. government out of near-bankruptcy.

What did workers do to fight for their rights?

While robber barons and other business leaders were busy getting rich, they were often doing so at the expense of the health, well-being, and sometimes even the lives of their workers. Most workers were on the job ten to fourteen hours a day, six days a week, and for little pay. Many, especially miners who worked underground with explosives, worked in unsafe conditions that claimed thousands of lives. Businessmen didn't give much thought to improving these conditions—they didn't need to. There were so many immigrants competing for jobs that any worker who complained could easily be replaced.

Railroad strikes, like this one in Baltimore, Maryland, shook America from coast to coast.

Since there was not much that one employee alone could do to improve conditions, workers slowly began to organize to make their voices heard. In 1877 railroad workers in West Virginia went on strike, refusing to work twelve-hour days after owners cut their already low pay. A wave of sympathetic strikes and demonstrations surged across the country in what became known as the Great Strike of 1877. Federal troops were called in to break up the protests, and by the time they were done, more than one hundred strikers had died.

While industry boomed, so did innovation and invention. Scores of things used every day, from the telephone to the electric lightbulb to Coca-Cola, were changing the way people lived and making lives more productive, enjoyable, and comfortable.

1852   Elisha Otis demonstrates a device that makes elevators safe, so that tall buildings become practical.

1876   Alexander Graham Bell invents the telephone.

1876   Thomas Alva Edison sets up the world's first "invention factory" in Menlo Park, New Jersey, where he invents the phonograph (1877), the electric lightbulb (1879), a movie camera and projector (1897), and so many other things that he registers an amazing 1,093 patents during his lifetime.

1880   George Eastman patents the first practical roll film for cameras.

1883   Brooklyn Bridge, the longest and highest of its day, opens over New York's East River.

1886   Cola syrup is accidentally mixed with carbonated water at a pharmacy in Atlanta, and Coca-Cola is born.

1894   Brothers John Harvey and Will Keith Kellogg invent cornflakes.

1903   Orville and Wilbur Wright fly the world's first motorized airplane.

1908   Henry Ford mass-produces Model T automobiles.

Why did farmers need to organize, too?

Factory workers weren't the only ones who were fed up with rule by the robber barons. Farmers were also at the mercy of things they couldn't control, including railroad rates, monopolies that made farm machinery, and loans from eastern banks. Local farmers' organizations called Granges pressed for reforms, but the Granges were largely powerless until they organized with city workers to form the People's, or Populist, Party.

The Populist Party united reformers from many different causes and areas of the country. Farmers from the South and West came together and joined laborers in the East. They wanted things like votes for women, prohibition of alcohol, an income tax, better prices for their crops, honest rates for loans, and government control of railroads. Populists believed the government was working for the rich and powerful, and they wanted a return to democracy. However, they were suspicious of foreigners and blacks and mainly wanted democracy for white, Protestant, native-born Americans.

The presidential election of 1896 was one of the most important in American history because it pitted Agriculture against Industry, the People against the Interests, the common man against the banker and speculator. In the end, the Republicans outspent the Democrats $7,000,000 to $300,000 in election campaigns, and Republican William McKinley beat William Jennings Bryan, a Populist who had won the Democratic nomination. But the Populists' ideas were not forgotten. They sparked the beginning of a long-awaited period of reform.

She's big, she's green, she's America's Welcome Queen. Who is she?

The Statue of Liberty (officially named Liberty Enlightening the World). For many immigrants who arrived in the United States after 1886, when the Statue of Liberty was unveiled, Lady Liberty was a thrilling first glimpse of America. She towered majestically over New York Harbor and nearby Ellis Island, offering hope to the new arrivals entering the island's inspection station. At Ellis Island, inspectors made immigrants pass health examinations and answer questions before they were allowed into the country. Those who had contagious diseases or the wrong papers were turned back. For good reason the island was known as the "isle of tears" or "heartbreak island" among immigrants.

Ellis Island was the country's main immigrant inspection station after 1892. Between 1892 and 1924, 16 million immigrants passed through its doors. They came at the height of a huge flood of newcomers—more than 30 million between 1820 and 1920—to the United States. Like those who'd come before them, immigrants arriving around the turn of the century were seeking jobs, homes, food, religious freedom, or escape from political wars in their homelands. Most who came through Ellis Island came from impoverished farms and towns in southern and eastern Europe. They scraped together money to travel as steerage passengers, crowded deep in the holds of the ship where the luggage was stored. Despite their poverty, the immigrants were not the "wretched refuse" Emma Lazarus described in her poem (see page 108). Most were energetic, resourceful people who helped make America what it is today.

❝WE LIVED THERE FOR THREE DAYS—MOTHER AND WE FIVE CHILDREN, THE YOUNGEST OF WHOM WAS THREE YEARS OLD. BECAUSE OF THE RIGOROUS PHYSICAL EXAMINATION THAT WE HAD TO SUBMIT TO, PARTICULARLY OF THE EYES, THERE WAS THIS TERRIBLE ANXIETY THAT ONE OF US MIGHT BE REJECTED. AND IF ONE OF US WAS, WHAT WOULD THE REST OF THE FAMILY DO? MY SISTER WAS INDEED MOMENTARILY REJECTED; SHE HAD BEEN SO ILL AND HAD CRIED SO MUCH THAT HER EYES WERE ABSOLUTELY BLOODSHOT, AND MOTHER WAS TOLD, 'WELL, WE CAN'T LET HER

IN.' BUT FORTUNATELY, MOTHER WAS AN INDOMITABLE SPIRIT AND FINALLY MADE THEM UNDERSTAND THAT IF HER CHILD HAD A FEW HOURS' REST AND A LITTLE BITE TO EAT SHE WOULD BE ALL RIGHT. IN THE END WE DID GET THROUGH. **99**

—Italian immigrant ANGELO PELLEGRINI, *who was about ten when his family was held at Ellis Island around 1913*

Where did turn-of-the-century immigrants make their new homes?

Often in cities, because many of the nation's vast open spaces had already been settled. In 1890, in fact, the Bureau of the Census declared that the frontier no longer existed. Of course, given the country's enormous size, there were still plenty of pockets of open land. But there were other reasons for settling in cities. Many immigrants didn't have the money to travel beyond their port of arrival. Cities also had more jobs, as well as *ghettos*, or ethnic neighborhoods, settled by people from the same country. The ghettos provided a sense of community and familiarity that helped newcomers adjust to the new nation's language, politics, and customs.

Still, urban areas were growing, and city life was crowded, loud, and dirty. Many immigrants lived in overflowing apartment buildings called *tenements*. Tenements were hot, dark, cramped, airless, and unhealthy, with as many as eight families sharing one bathroom. To make matters worse, many were used as small factories, or "sweatshops," where immigrant families worked long hours to make a scanty living doing jobs like rolling cigars, assembling silk flowers, or shelling nuts.

⭐ A reporter named Jacob Riis was just one of many reformers who helped those in the tenements. Riis, himself a Danish immigrant, wrote about and photographed many newly arrived immigrants who were struggling for survival in tenements and on the streets of New York City. His 1890 book of photographs, *How the Other Half Lives*, helped convince politicians to pass laws that improved conditions for the poor.

Jane Addams

Jane Addams(left) and fellow advocate Mary McDowell campaign for peace.

Jane Addams (1860–1935) was a courageous and determined social reformer whose work on behalf of women, children, and immigrants made her the most admired American woman of her day.

Born to a wealthy family in Illinois, Addams was among the first generation of American women to go to college. After graduating from Rockford Female Seminary in 1881, Addams traveled to Europe and was inspired by a settlement house she visited in London. In 1889 Addams moved to the slums of Chicago and founded America's first settlement house, Hull House. At Hull House Chicago's immigrants could learn to read and speak English, take art lessons, watch or perform entertainment, get child care, and join sports clubs. Hull House was so successful that four hundred other settlement houses soon opened around the country.

Addams did not stop there. She worked to clean up the neighborhood around Hull House (even taking a job as garbage inspector) and to improve labor laws and the juvenile justice system. On a national level, Addams served as vice president of the National American Woman Suffrage Association (NAWSA), advocating women's right to vote. She was also a founder of the American Civil Liberties Union (ACLU) and the National Association for the Advancement of Colored People (NAACP). During World War I, Addams campaigned at home and abroad for world peace. Though many Americans said Addams's pacifism was unpatriotic, in 1931 she became the first American woman to receive the Nobel Peace Prize.

What did many new immigrants face, in the midst of their other troubles?

Racism and discrimination. And believe it or not, it often came from other immigrants. Because there weren't enough jobs for everyone, friction arose between newly arrived immigrants and those who had been in America longer. Immigrants who had just arrived were generally willing to work longer hours and for less money, and more established immigrants didn't appreciate the competition. They didn't stop to think that it wasn't so long ago that they, or their relatives, had been the newcomers.

Racism and discrimination were common around the turn of the century, and not just among immigrants. Those hit worst of all were the Chinese, about three hundred thousand of whom had arrived on the West Coast since the California gold rush. In 1882 Congress passed the Chinese Exclusion Act, stopping almost all Chinese immigration. (This was especially unfair considering how hard the Chinese had worked on the railroad and in mines to help the country.) In 1924 another law limited the number of Jews, Italians, and Eastern Europeans who could enter the United States. Immigrants from Great Britain and Germany, however, whose ancestors had been in America longer, were much more welcome.

What was Jim Crow up to toward the end of the nineteenth century?

Jim Crow was coming back in a big way. (Remember Jim Crow laws? They made segregation between whites and blacks legal.) In 1875 Congress passed a civil rights act to end Jim Crow laws, but the Supreme Court overturned the act in 1883. That made racial segregation legal again.

⭐ In the South taxes at voting places, literacy tests, and even threats and violence wiped out the voting rights black men had won with the Fifteenth Amendment. Sometimes tests for black voters included questions like, "How many bubbles are there in a bar of soap?" Those who failed were not allowed to vote.

Jim Crow survived because, in many ways, Reconstruction had failed. As the country got swept up in incredible economic growth, the old South began to reemerge, and blacks were sometimes worse off than they'd been before the war. Not only did they face segregation, they feared for their lives. Between the 1880s and the 1960s, *white supremacists*, or people who believed that whites were superior to everyone else, lynched more than 4,700 people (more than 3,400 of them black), in the North and West as well as the South.

In 1896 the Court reinforced Jim Crow laws in a case called *Plessy v. Ferguson*. Homer Plessy, who was only one-eighth black and therefore looked white, wanted to show how foolish racial categories were. To test the idea that separate facilities could still be equal, Plessy sat in the white section of a railroad car. He was promptly arrested and jailed. Though he and his lawyers said "separate but equal" was unconstitutional, all the courts, right on up to the Supreme Court, disagreed. The verdict in *Plessy v. Ferguson* set the stage for legal discrimination.

What did prominent blacks think should be done about racial discrimination?

They couldn't agree. One popular black leader was Booker T. Washington (1856–1915). He was a former slave who went to school during Reconstruction and then became the first head of Alabama's Tuskegee Institute, the nation's major industrial training school for blacks. Washington was a talented, commanding speaker. He said that blacks should get ahead by working hard and getting an education. He believed that if blacks could use these skills to gain economic equality, then they could move on to other forms of equal rights.

Many Americans admired and respected Booker T. Washington. But a few thought he accepted Jim Crow laws too easily. One was a man named W.E.B. DuBois (1868–1963). DuBois was the first black to earn a doctoral degree from Harvard University. He was an agitator, not a compromiser. DuBois wanted nothing less than full equality for blacks. He also worked for better treatment for immigrants and Jews and for the vote for women. In 1909 he cofounded the NAACP, which had both black and white members and became a major force in the fight for civil rights for blacks.

How many different uses for the peanut can you come up with?

At Tuskegee Institute a black inventor, teacher, and agricultural chemist named George Washington Carver (1864?–1943) invented more than three hundred! Decades of growing cotton had hurt southern soil, so Carver encouraged farmers to grow things that would enrich the earth instead, like peanuts, sweet potatoes, and soybeans. To make these crops more profitable, he invented ways to use them in plastics, dyes, soaps, rubber, medicines, and molasses. (Though he didn't invent peanut butter, as many people believe.) Carver's experiments and inventions brought new life to the slow economy of the South.

★★★★ CHAPTER 7 *★★★★*

America Builds an Empire

"America cannot be an ostrich with its head in the sand."

—PRESIDENT WOODROW WILSON, *February 1, 1916*

What was America's "splendid little war"?

The Spanish-American War of 1898, fought to help Cuba win its independence from Spain and to protect U.S. business interests on the island.

In 1898 Cuba (an island off the coast of Florida) was a colony of Spain. Its rulers were so cruel and corrupt that the Cuban people finally rose up against them. Immediately two American newspapers that were competing for readers began printing sensational stories about the atrocities Spaniards were committing against Cubans. When William Randolph Hearst of the *New York Journal* and Joseph Pulitzer of the *New York World* couldn't find a story, they made one up. (Hearst cabled his artist in Cuba, who wanted to come home because he said there was no war: "Please remain. You furnish the pictures and I'll furnish the war.") This invented or exaggerated reporting is called "yellow journalism." It made Americans cry out for war with Spain to help the Cubans win their independence, even though some just wanted to gain control of the island and protect U.S. business interests there.

President William McKinley didn't want a war. But it was hard to avoid after the U.S. battleship *Maine*, on a visit to Cuba to protect Americans and their property, mysteriously exploded in Cuba's Havana harbor on February 15, 1898, killing 260 American sailors. Spanish authorities said the explosion came from an accident aboard the ship. (Today this is generally thought to be what happened.) But Americans who wanted war blamed Spain.

"Remember the *Maine!*" cried the newspapers. President McKinley gave in to public opinion and went to war in April.

The war was over in just 113 days. Cuba won limited independence from Spain. In its peace treaty with Spain, the United States gained the formerly Spanish territories of Guam, Puerto Rico, Wake Island, and the Philippines. At about the same time, American settlers in Hawaii, having overthrown Hawaii's Queen Liliuokalani in 1893, asked the U.S. government to annex the Hawaiian Islands, and it did. (By *annexing*, the U.S. government incorporated the islands into its territory. Hawaii became the fiftieth state in 1959.) All these new acquisitions helped build up American strength, as they provided military bases in other parts of the world. The United States emerged from the Spanish-American War a major world power.

★ The Spanish-American war made a national hero of future vice president and president Theodore Roosevelt. Roosevelt was the assistant secretary of the navy when war broke out, but he was so eager to get into the action that he resigned his position and organized a group of cavalrymen who called themselves "Rough Riders." After a few weeks of training, the Rough Riders boarded their ship for Cuba. When they found there wasn't enough room on board for their horses, they renamed themselves the "Weary Walkers" and marched into battle. Two days after Roosevelt led his men to victory at the Battle of San Juan Hill, the Americans crushed the Spanish fleet and brought an end to the war.

Why did President Theodore Roosevelt carry a big stick?

He didn't actually carry one, but the African proverb "Speak softly, and carry a big stick" was Teddy Roosevelt's favorite saying. It was also the principle by which he often ran the country.

Theodore Roosevelt (1858–1919) became the youngest president in American history when an *anarchist* named Leon Czolgosz assassinated President McKinley in 1901. (An anarchist is someone who doesn't believe in government.) Forty-two-year-old Roosevelt was probably the country's most active, spirited leader ever. Sometimes after a busy day at the White House, Teddy jogged around the Washington Monument to work off extra energy. As president, Roosevelt put his massive energies into demanding better conditions for Americans. He and other "Progressives" like him wanted to give working people more protection against big business, which had gotten bigger and more powerful by combining into even larger businesses, called *trusts*. Trusts, like monopolies, were bad for the average person because they made everything more expensive. Workers couldn't find better-paying jobs because all the jobs were controlled by a few people who kept labor unions out, often with the help of armed guards. By 1890 average people had complained enough that Congress passed the first law to control these businesses, the Sherman Anti-Trust Act. But few politicians wanted to use it against the powerful robber barons until Teddy Roosevelt came along. He was the first to enforce the law, and became known as a trustbuster. Roosevelt was not out to bust all the trusts, but he thought that the people needed what he called a "square deal."

Teddy had his flaws. He believed that "civilized" countries like the United States deserved to control "barbarous" countries. He promoted the racist idea that white Americans should have more children to "strengthen" the country. Still, Roosevelt did do many things to make life better for the average American. He was a passionate nature lover who did more than any other president to preserve America's natural resources. He

established five national parks and protected more than 150 million acres of national forests. Roosevelt also protected Americans' health by urging Congress to pass the Meat Inspection Act and the Pure Food and Drug Act, after a novel by Upton Sinclair called *The Jungle* described the spoiled and contaminated food sold by the meat-packing industry.

❝A MAN COULD RUN HIS HANDS OVER THE PILES OF MEAT AND SWAP OFF HANDFULS OF DRY DUNG OF RATS. THESE RATS WERE NUISANCES, AND THE PACKERS WOULD PUT OUT POISONED BREAD FOR THEM; THEY WOULD DIE; AND THE RATS, BREAD, AND MEAT WOULD GO IN THE HOPPERS TOGETHER. THIS IS NO FAIRY STORY AND NO JOKE; THE MEAT WOULD BE SHOVELED INTO CARTS, AND THE MAN WHO DID THE SHOVELING DID NOT TROUBLE TO LIFT OUT A RAT, EVEN WHEN HE SAW ONE.❞

—UPTON SINCLAIR, *The Jungle, 1906*

⭐ For nearly a century American boys have learned to "be prepared" by becoming Boy Scouts. The Boy Scouts of America, modeled on Boy Scouts in Britain, was incorporated by Chicago publisher William Boyce in 1910. Then, as now, scouts were taught to be self-reliant, physically fit, capable in the wilderness, and stewards of the environment. British Boy Scouts also inspired Girl Guides, an organization brought to the United States in 1912 by Juliette Gordon Low of Savannah, Georgia. (Girl Guides became Girl Scouts by 1915.) Similar to Boy Scouts, Girl Scouts promoted service, patriotism, and self-respect. Low taught her first members household skills and civics lessons but also took them hiking and camping. Today millions of American Boy Scouts and Girl Scouts earn merit badges in such varied activities as oceanography, computer programming, photography, wood carving, and martial arts.

What did President Roosevelt do with 7,800 miles?

He got rid of them—for anyone traveling by boat between the Atlantic and Pacific Oceans, that is. Roosevelt arranged for the building of a canal through Central America so ships wouldn't

Building the canal in 1906

have to sail nearly eight thousand miles around South America to get from the Atlantic to the Pacific. The Panama Canal was originally supposed to cut through Colombia, but Colombia refused to sell the land. A U.S.-sponsored revolt by independence fighters in Colombia quickly led to the creation of a new country, Panama, which leased the Canal Zone to the United States. (Panama took control of the land and canal in 2000.)

Digging the canal was horrendous work. Panama is a land of tremendous tropical heat, dense jungle, and mosquitoes that carry deadly yellow fever. Nearly six thousand workers died building the canal, most of them from disease. Finally, after eleven years of shoveling, a trip from the Atlantic to the Pacific that once took four months took about forty-seven days.

Roosevelt pushed for the canal because he wanted the U.S. navy to be able to move quickly from one ocean to the other. He had built up a powerful navy and sent it on a cruise around the world as a parade of American power—the "big stick" of international affairs. President Roosevelt helped make America a world leader in other ways. For instance, he worked out a peace deal between Russia and Japan during the Russo-Japanese War (1904–5). It was rare in those days for a U.S. president to be so active in international affairs. For his efforts he became the first American to win a Nobel prize when he was awarded the Nobel Peace Prize in 1906.

The start of the twentieth century brought amazing advancements around the world. The telephone, invented by Alexander Graham Bell in 1876, finally went into widespread use by the turn of the century. And in 1901 Italian inventor Guglielmo Marconi showed what radio signals could do when he sent Morse code for the letter S across the Atlantic from England to Canada. Nineteen years later, the first commercial American radio station, KDKA of Pittsburgh, went on the air.

Henry Ford invented the automobile.

False. But Henry Ford (1863–1947) was the first to make cars on an assembly line, which made them affordable for the average American. Since the invention of the "horseless carriage" in the late 1800s, cars had been a novelty item that only the rich could afford. But Ford wanted to make cars for the masses. In 1908, after he'd been in business for five years, Ford introduced the Model T. Instead of being made by hand one at a time, the Model T was made on a moving assembly line using interchangeable parts. The efficiency of his methods cut the cost of a Model T from $850 in 1908 to $440 in 1915. Eventually his factories turned out one Model T every twenty-four seconds!

Ford's democratic car changed the nation. People who had never been beyond their hometowns could get out and see the country. A network of roads began to unite the United States, and motels, service stations, and eventually supermarkets sprang up. More suburbs grew up around cities because people could drive to work. First Ford, and then other employers, began paying better wages. They did this both to keep their workers from walking off their monotonous assembly-line jobs, and also as a way of creating their own consumers. (If employees made enough money, they could buy the cars they made.)

GREAT AMERICAN PASTIMES
What did Americans think about being in the driver's seat?

Driving quickly became a passion, almost a sport, among auto-owning Americans early in the 1900s. It wasn't always about reaching a destination, but about taking the drive itself. Few owners of early horseless carriages seemed to mind that going for a drive through the countryside could be a messy affair: Unpaved roads and the cars' lack of windshields meant motorists had to put on goggles, veils, and *dusters*, or long overcoats that protected clothing.

How did the death of a European archduke start the first world war?

In 1914 a Serbian assassin killed Austrian Archduke Franz Ferdinand, heir to the Austrian throne. That provided a convenient excuse for Austria-Hungary, which wanted to take over its smaller neighbor, to declare war on Serbia. One by one, other countries in Europe, Asia, North Africa, and eventually North America joined the fight in support of one side or the other. This Great War (it wasn't called World War I until a second world war came along twenty years later) was the first war to involve countries from all over the world.

The seeds of war had been growing for decades. Fueled by the Industrial Revolution, the powerful countries of Europe had become hungrier than ever for power, territory, and money. Some had created huge colonial empires that stretched around the globe. Some had built up their military forces and made protective alliances with other countries. France, Great Britain, and Russia formed the Triple Entente (also called the Allies); Germany, Austria-Hungary, and Italy signed the Triple Alliance (also called the Central Powers). If one country was attacked, the others on its side pledged to defend it. Though the alliances were meant to keep peace, they were a recipe for war.

No one had imagined the incredible bloodiness and destruction made possible by new weapons like tanks, machine guns, grenades, long-range artillery, submarines, airplanes, and poison gas. Before the war was over in 1918, about 10 million soldiers had died worldwide. An additional 20 million people died of hunger, disease, and other war-related causes, and 6 million were left crippled. America's share of the casualties was 117,000 dead from combat and disease.

Why did the United States enter World War I?

When the war broke out in Europe, the United States declared that it would remain neutral. President Woodrow Wilson urged Americans not to take sides, but so many had deep roots in Europe that it was difficult not to. Most Americans sided with the Allies, especially after German submarines sank a British passenger ship called the *Lusitania* in 1915. Almost 1,200 people went down with the ship, including 128 Americans. There was a brief clamor for war right after the incident, but most Americans supported President Wilson's neutrality.

Yet in 1917 newspapers published a telegram sent by Germany's foreign minister, Arthur Zimmermann, which revealed that Germany was trying to lure Mexico into the Central Powers and turn it against the United States. The Zimmermann telegram left President Wilson with little choice but to ask Congress to declare war.

AMERICAN VOICES

66 THE WORLD MUST BE MADE SAFE FOR DEMOCRACY. . . . WE HAVE NO SELFISH ENDS TO SERVE. WE DESIRE NO CONQUEST, NO DOMINION. WE SEEK NO INDEMNITIES FOR OURSELVES, NO MATERIAL COMPENSATION FOR THE SACRIFICES WE SHALL FREELY MAKE. WE ARE BUT ONE OF THE CHAMPIONS OF THE RIGHTS OF MANKIND. . . . 99

—PRESIDENT WILSON, *from his address to Congress, April 2, 1917, asking for a declaration of war against Germany*

Wilson's speech was met with thunderous applause. Afterward the president told an aide, "My message today was a message of death for our young men. How strange it seems to applaud that." Then he went back to his office, put his head on his desk, and wept.

By the time the United States entered the war, the Allies were on their last legs, with France and Britain drawing on their last resources. The addition of fresh American soldiers helped turn the tide of war by the end of 1918. Germany, the last of the Central Powers to surrender to the Allies, did so at the "Eleventh Hour"—11 A.M. on the eleventh day of the eleventh month of the year. Around the world November 11 became known as Armistice Day to honor veterans of World War I. In America the name was later changed to Veterans' Day to honor soldiers of all wars.

MAJOR MILESTONES IN WORLD WAR I
1914–1918

1914

JUNE 28   A Serbian nationalist murders Archduke Franz Ferdinand of Austria in Sarajevo. Austria-Hungary declares war on Serbia, its tiny southern neighbor, five days later.

AUGUST 1–23   Germany declares war on Russia and France; Britain declares war on Germany; Austria-Hungary declares war on Russia; Japan declares war on Germany.

SEPTEMBER 5   In the Battle of the Marne, the first major battle of the war, Germany tries to take Paris before the Allies can fully mobilize. The French and British repulse the German invasion. This squelches Germany's plans for a quick victory and begins three years of horrific, stalemated trench warfare in which soldiers spend months in bloody, muddy ditches, trying to hide from—but also kill—an enemy that is doing the same thing. Casualties top 250,000 on each side.

OCTOBER 29   Turkey enters the war against the Allies. Italy remains neutral.

1915

MAY 7   A German submarine sinks British passenger liner *Lusitania*, killing almost 1,200, including 128 Americans.

MAY 23   Italy joins the Allies.

1916

JUNE 16   President Wilson is nominated for a second term and wins reelection under the slogan "He Kept Us Out of War."

JULY–NOVEMBER   In one of the most disastrous battles of the war, British troops attack German trenches in the Battle of the Somme. Britain makes little or no territorial gains yet suffers the worst casualties in its history—420,000 men. The French lose 195,000; the Germans, 650,000.

1917

FEBRUARY 24   The British Secret Service intercepts the Zimmermann telegram, revealing Germany's attempt to lure Mexico into the Central Powers.

APRIL 2   President Wilson asks Congress to declare war on Germany.

1918

JUNE 25   American soldiers, untested in battle on European soil, prove their ability by capturing the forest of Belleau Wood from the Germans.

SEPTEMBER 26   American troops join Allied forces on the offensive at the Battle of Argonne Forest, the last major battle of the war. The German army falls back and begins to collapse.

NOVEMBER 11   Germany signs a peace agreement and fighting ends.

1919

JANUARY 28   The Treaty of Versailles is signed in France.

What were President Wilson's "Fourteen Points"?

They were a generous and forgiving end to the war that President Wilson hoped would ensure "peace without victory," a lasting peace in which no country was blamed, humiliated, or made to pay for a war that everyone had started. Wilson felt that a harsh peace treaty would only make the defeated Central Powers—especially Germany—angry, poor, and unstable. His Fourteen Points tried to deal with the issues that had really started the war in the first place, calling for freedom of the seas, an end to secret pacts among nations, fewer weapons, and a League of Nations to serve as a peacekeeping force to help avoid future conflicts.

Unfortunately, however, some of Wilson's most important points were pushed aside in the negotiations for the Treaty of Versailles. The rest of the Allies were angry about the massive property destruction and loss of life caused by the war, and they wanted Germany to pay for it. So they slapped Germany, Austria, and Turkey with huge *reparation* payments, or rebuilding costs. Those countries were forced to give up land in Eastern Europe, the Middle East, and Africa. Germany also had to accept responsibility for starting the war. The harsh punishments inflicted on Germany left the country poor and angry. Altogether, the Treaty of Versailles was a formula for disaster—specifically, another world war.

★ In 1919 President Wilson suffered a *stroke*, or brain damage caused by a blood clot, while touring the country. Wilson was bedridden and incapable of doing much. While he recovered, First Lady Edith Wilson made it seem as though she was just bringing papers to her husband when she was actually making presidential decisions for him. At that time Wilson could have resigned, but his doctors told the First Lady that he might lose his will to live if he did. Mrs. Wilson was both criticized and ridiculed as the "presidentress" who was running a "petticoat government." In 1967 Congress amended the Constitution to allow the vice president to take over temporarily if the president is unable to perform his duties. George Bush became the first "acting president" for a few hours when Ronald Reagan had surgery in 1985.

Why were Americans so scared of the color red after the war?

It wasn't the color but what it stood for: Communism.

Communism is an economic system in which the government owns almost all the land, industry, and business; controls work; and gives out goods according to need instead of according to how hard a person works. Communism is usually paired with a totalitarian government, where the leader has total control. These forces, under the leadership of dictator Vladimir Lenin and his successor, Joseph Stalin, came to rule Russia during World War I. Russia then merged with several neighboring republics and formed the larger Union of Soviet Socialist Republics (USSR), or Soviet Union. Many Americans were scared that Communists, or "Reds" (named after the color of their flag), would take over the United States. They also feared anarchists. These

USSR dictator Stalin (center) at the Sixth Party Congress in 1930

two groups, though unrelated, were lumped together because both seemed to threaten the American way of life.

Americans were suspicious because, after World War I, the United States was a turbulent place. During the war, prices had gone up, and many factory workers didn't feel their wages were keeping up with inflation. Unhappy workers, looking for someone to blame for their troubles, turned their frustration against foreigners, especially Russians.

After a series of bombs targeted famous Americans like J. P. Morgan and Attorney General A. Mitchell Palmer, Palmer unleashed a "Red Scare" against those he thought were dangerous or undesirable. He ordered the arrest of six thousand suspected Reds on one night, six hundred of whom were deported to other countries. Soon thereafter, in 1921 and again in 1924, the government cut the number of immigrants allowed into the country.

⭐ Perhaps the most famous casualties of the Red Scare were two Italian immigrants, Nicola Sacco and Bartolomeo Vanzetti. Sacco and Vanzetti were known anarchists who were arrested in 1920 and accused of robbery and murder. They were tried and convicted, and eventually executed for crimes that, even today, no one is sure they committed. (Years later, reports showed that Sacco was probably guilty and Vanzetti probably innocent.) Many people said it was their radical beliefs that were really on trial.

Harry Houdini

Harry Houdini (1874–1926), one of the greatest escape artists of all time, was an immigrant who succeeded in a uniquely American way—through showmanship. His real name was Ehrich Weisz. He was a rabbi's son, born in Budapest, Hungary, but raised in Appleton, Wisconsin, and New York City. (Later in life, Houdini hid his foreign birth and told everyone he was born in Wisconsin.) Houdini's family was poor. To help out, he began working, delivering newspapers and shining shoes at the age of eight. But Houdini was supremely ambitious and wanted more from life than unrecognized labor. Changing his name to sound more like a magician, he began performing simple magic tricks in his teens. By 1900 he moved on to the act that would make him famous: Houdini, the master of escape.

Houdini escaped from handcuffs, straitjackets (while dangling from skyscrapers), huge milk cans, chain-wrapped boxes underwater, and just about anything anyone could think of. He was a terrific showman. His colorful posters, plastered all over any city where he appeared, called him the "Master Mystifier," the "King of Handcuffs," the "Greatest Necromancer of the Age." "Nothing on Earth can hold Houdini a prisoner," the posters boasted. In the 1920s he even starred in a number of early movies. Although he was a terrible actor, he understood that movies were the wave of the future. When he died in 1926, the most successful entertainer of his time, the whole world mourned.

Did birds make the Great Migration?

Not the Great Migration of the early twentieth century. The migrators then were southern blacks, who left the South for a chance at a better life in northern cities. At the turn of the century, almost 90 percent of the country's black population lived in the South. But when World War I broke out, the economy boomed and many jobs opened up in the factories of the North. By 1920 up to 2 million black families had moved to cities such as Detroit and Chicago. The Great Migration continued through most of the century, and by 1970 only 53 percent of blacks still lived in the South.

What was prohibited during Prohibition?

The making and selling of alcoholic beverages—beer, wine, and hard liquor. The ideas of prohibition and *temperance,* or prohibiting the drinking of alcohol, had been around since colonial times. But they gained momentum in the 1870s, especially in the West and Midwest where so many saloons sprang up during the cowboy era.

In 1874 the Women's Christian Temperance Union (WCTU) was founded to end, or at least control, alcohol consumption and the evils that often went along with it. The WCTU became one of the most powerful reform groups of the Progressive Era. Its members fought not only against alcohol but for health and education reform and for the vote for women. Together with the more militant protests of anti-alcohol activist Carry A. Nation—who swung her hatchet through saloons in Kansas, smashing everything in her way—the WCTU pushed for the Eighteenth Amendment, passed in 1919. That amendment made Prohibition the law of the land.

End of story? Not at all. Prohibition was supposed to make Americans more moral, but instead it made them less so. Many people simply didn't view drinking as a crime, and most went on drinking. Prohibition created a nation of lawbreakers. Illegal "rumrunners" and "bootleggers" transported and sold liquor to "speakeasies," or secret bars that pretended to be businesses like barbershops or banks. It was the heyday of organized crime, which made big money controlling the bootleg market. And although drinking per person decreased, new people picked up the habit because now that it was illegal, it was also cool. Women and younger people decided to try it.

No one had expected these things to happen. In 1933 the Twenty-first Amendment repealed the Eighteenth Amendment, and Prohibition was over.

⭐ One of the most notorious leaders of organized crime in the 1920s was Chicago gangster Al Capone. Capone's band of criminals carried out illegal activities in exchange for money and the protection of other gang members. Capone dominated the bootleg market by murdering and terrorizing the competition, crimes he got away with by bribing police officers and other officials. In 1932 Capone was sent to jail for not paying his taxes.

What more lasting reform did women achieve in 1920?

Since the Seneca Falls Convention in 1848, the campaign for women's *suffrage*, or the right to vote, had become more visible. Younger women had joined the movement and introduced new ways of making themselves heard, like speaking out in public rallies and organizing suffrage parades. Involvement in organizations like the WCTU had taught women to speak up and had reinforced the power of working together on a national level.

In the years leading up to 1920, there were two major national suffrage organizations. The NAWSA had been the group of Elizabeth Cady Stanton and Susan B. Anthony. Now led by Carrie Chapman Catt, the NAWSA worked to get the vote at both the national level and in each state. The other group was the more radical National Woman's Party (NWP), which worked solely to win the vote on the federal level.

Members of the NWP put plenty of suffering in the fight for suffrage (though the word *suffrage* comes from the Latin *suffragium* for "vote"). Inspired by British suffragettes, who chained themselves to buildings, blew up mailboxes, and started riots, NWP leader Alice Paul organized daily protests outside the White House. During World War I, the women protested the contradiction that America was fighting for democracy abroad, yet American women didn't have full democracy at home. Police arrested many of these *suffragists* (the American term for suffragettes), and several, including Alice Paul, protested by going on hunger strikes in jail.

Alice Paul raises the suffrage flag after the Nineteenth Amendment is ratified.

In 1918 Montana representative Jeannette Rankin, the first woman elected to Congress, introduced a bill for a constitutional suffrage amendment. By 1920 Congress and thirty-five of the thirty-six states necessary for ratification had approved the bill. Tennessee made it thirty-six when the state legislature approved the bill by just one vote—after a young representative received a letter from his mother urging him to be a "good boy, and help Mrs. Catt put the 'Rat' in ratification."

How did a scandal called Teapot Dome get President Warren G. Harding into a lot of hot water?

President Warren G. Harding, who won election in 1920 after campaigning for a postwar "return to normalcy," was very popular during his presidency. Since then, though, he has become less so. Harding's administration was entangled in many scandals, the most famous of which involved oil reserves at Teapot Dome, Wyoming.

Teapot Dome was one of two oil-rich areas Congress had set aside for government use, to make sure the military would have enough oil reserves in case of an emergency. Even though the oil was meant for public use, men from Harding's administration secretly gave rights to the land to private developers, who then got rich drilling the oil. (Harding's men got rich in the process, too.) The president had been betrayed. Harding died in 1923, while the scandal was being uncovered.

Scandal-ridden Harding hadn't exactly achieved "normalcy," but his successor, President Calvin Coolidge, would fare a little better. "Silent Cal" was honest, quiet, and ran a hands-off government. "The chief business of America is business," Coolidge said. Then he stood back and let business do its thing.

Why were the twenties "roaring"?

The 1920s were unlike any previous decade in American history; they were the beginning of the modern age. Movies, radio, cars, airplanes, and a new music called jazz all took off, as the pace of life exploded in a frenzy of new sounds, images, activities, and opportunities. The economy was roaring, the stock market was booming, and more Americans were better off than ever before.

Jazz music, a uniquely American art form, started in New Orleans in the early 1900s. But it was in the twenties that it spread to other cities, popularized by musicians and singers like Louis Armstrong, Bessie Smith, and Duke Ellington. With jazz came wild dance crazes like the Charleston, whose rapid pace reflected the new tempo of American life. New fashions also arrived on the scene, as women's hemlines (which had always reached the ankle) went up, up, up. Some young women called "flappers" wore these shorter skirts, short bobbed hair, and lipstick, all of which shocked the older generations. Flappers were modern. They danced and drove cars, and some even smoked and drank illegal liquor.

With more leisure time and money to spend, Americans built amusement parks and flocked to the movies. People started playing tennis and golf and began a love affair with organized sports, especially baseball and its most lovable, larger-than-life player, Babe Ruth. Sports, as well as concerts, nightly news, entertainment, and advertisements, came into American living rooms for the first time via the radio. Literature flourished as writer F. Scott Fitzgerald captured the party atmosphere of the "Jazz Age" (a term he coined) in *The Great Gatsby*, while Ernest Hemingway wrote books about the Great War. Art, literature, and music thrived in New York's Harlem neighborhood during a wave of creativity that came to be known as the "Harlem Renaissance." Black writers like the poet Langston Hughes and the novelist Zora Neale Hurston gained recognition and praise for writing about the black experience.

AMERICAN ENGLISH

Jazz, that uniquely American word, may have its roots in Africa. People who study language guess that *jazz* started as a West African word, then entered English in the early 1900s as black slang meaning any energetic activity. The word gradually came to mean the lively music played by black musicians in the South. Now, as an adjective (*jazzy*), a verb phrase (*to jazz up*), and a noun with a completely different meaning (*all that jazz*), it has made the language even richer.

Why was "Lucky Lindy" so lucky?

Americans were flying high in the twenties, and they found a perfect hero in "Lucky Lindy," aviator Charles Lindbergh (1902–1974). Lindbergh became the first person to fly *solo* (alone) across the Atlantic Ocean in 1927, when flying was still highly dangerous. Young, handsome, daring, modest, and skillful, Lindbergh charmed the world when he made his historic flight from New York to Paris in 33½ hours. Upon his return to the United States, Lindbergh's adoring countrymen gave him a ticker-tape parade so huge it produced more confetti than was thrown to greet the troops returning from World War I.

Within two years of Lindbergh's flight, most airmail airlines were carrying passengers. Lindbergh helped found a passenger airline company and flew all over the world. But within a few years, his celebrity status would make him "Unlucky Lindy": A kidnapper tried to profit from his fame by taking his twenty-month-old baby, who was later found dead.

Another famous flyer of Lindbergh's era was Amelia Earhart (1897–1937). In 1932 Earhart repeated Lindbergh's feat of flying solo across the Atlantic. But during a flight around the world in 1937, her plane went down over the South Pacific. No one has ever found any trace of her.

While Charles Lindbergh was realizing the possibilities of air travel, a physicist named Robert Goddard (1882–1945) was experimenting with the possibilities of space travel. Goddard wanted to send a rocket to the moon. At the time many people thought that idea was more than a little crazy. But Goddard, who started designing rockets when he was still in school, is now known as the "father of American rocketry." He experimented with different fuels and, in 1926, launched the first liquid-fueled rocket from his aunt's strawberry farm in Massachusetts. The rocket rose only forty-one feet in the air, about as high as the top of a two-story house, but it was the beginning of a journey to the moon—and beyond. By the 1930s one of his rockets had gone a mile above the earth.

CHAPTER 8

Fearing Fear from the Thirties to the Forties

"This generation of Americans has a rendezvous with destiny."

—FRANKLIN D. ROOSEVELT, *June 27, 1936*

What was so great about the Great Depression?

It wasn't Great meaning "terrific"; it was Great meaning "enormous." A *depression* is an extreme slowdown in the economy, when business activity and prices fall and unemployment rises. The Great Depression was the largest and longest depression in American history. At least 13 million workers, one-quarter of the work force, lost their jobs. Many of those who were still employed had to take drastic pay cuts. More than five thousand banks closed, taking their customers' life savings with them. Huge numbers of businesses and factories closed, too, without the banks to loan them money. This meant fewer jobs, which meant fewer people buying goods, which meant more factories had to shut down. And downward it spiraled, spreading through Europe and other parts of the world.

There were several reasons the Great Depression was more devastating than those the nation had been through before. In previous depressions most of the population lived on farms and could grow food to survive. Now most people lived in cities and couldn't do that. Yet the factory jobs were growing fewer because human workers were being replaced by machines.

Machines changed things in another way. New equipment and technology had made factories more efficient. Businesses that wanted to grow sold *stock*, or shares of ownership in their corporations. When a corporation does well, stockholders share in the profits. In the twenties people poured their money into the stock market and stock prices went way up. The value of some stocks doubled, or even tripled, in a matter of days. Americans were so confident of the stock market that some pulled their savings out of banks or borrowed money to buy stock. So many people invested in the market that stock prices became artificially high. Americans seemed wealthy, but their wealth was only on paper.

On October 29, 1929—"Black Tuesday"—the business bubble burst. Stock values plunged. Suddenly everyone wanted to sell, but no one wanted to buy. Many people lost their life savings almost overnight and were left with nothing but debt and loans they couldn't repay. The party of the Roaring Twenties was over.

Did the stock market crash cause the Great Depression?

No. The stock market crash on Black Tuesday marked the beginning of the Great Depression, but it did not cause it. The crash was a symptom of an economy that was already sick. The problems had started during the postwar industrial boom, when businesses built bigger factories and were soon making more goods than they could sell. Still, many people went into debt buying gadgets and stocks on credit.

Farmers, too, had surpluses because they had become more productive during World War I to help feed starving Europeans. But after the war, when Europe's farmers were back at work, American farmers kept producing just as much food. Crop prices fell and thousands of farmers went bankrupt, even while they were surrounded by their harvests. They couldn't afford to buy what the factories had too much of, and factory workers couldn't afford to buy their excess crops. In this agonizing situation, the government was no help because it didn't have the power to control these parts of the economy.

Why did President Herbert Hoover have so many towns named after him during the Great Depression?

Because so many people blamed him for the depression.

President Herbert Hoover was a self-made millionaire. In a speech before his election in 1928, Hoover talked about the "rugged individualism" and self-reliance that he felt had made American progress possible. He believed that it wasn't the government's place to help people out of their difficulties. Even after the stock market crash, the president kept an optimistic view, saying in 1930, "Business and industry have turned the corner." To be sure, there was no way to predict the depth of the depression, since things had never been so bad before. But the situation just kept getting worse. By 1933 thousands of Americans who had been evicted from their homes were living in "Hoovervilles," or shantytowns full of shelters made of scrap lumber and boxes.

President Hoover actually did do much more than people give him credit for. He started the largest public works projects in American history to provide jobs, and he had the government lend money to banks, insurance companies, railroads, and state governments to keep them from going bankrupt. But most of his efforts were too little too late.

What was the dust bowl?

a) a superdry area of the Great Plains in the 1930s

b) a football game for teams that didn't qualify for the Rose Bowl

c) a dish that hasn't been used in a very long time

The answer is letter *a*. Great Plains farmers were hit especially hard by the Great Depression. Not only had their crop prices fallen (sometimes to below what it cost to grow them), but they were also devastated by the worst drought of the century. Their already overworked soil, where hardy prairie grasses had been replaced by wheat, was so dry that it broke down into a fine dust and blew away in huge clouds. The worst of the "dust bowl" was in Oklahoma, but Kansas, Colorado, New Mexico, and Texas were also affected. More than 3 million people left the Great Plains during the 1930s, forced off the land because they couldn't grow crops or make payments on their farms. These "Oakies" (so-called because most came from Oklahoma) loaded up their old trucks with pots, pans, suitcases, washtubs, and mattresses and moved to cities in search of work, or to find seasonal jobs as migrant workers in California. A journalist of the era named John Steinbeck interviewed many "Oakies" in California and then wrote about their plight in a famous novel called *The Grapes of Wrath*.

"LAST WEEKEND WAS THE WORST DUST STORM WE EVER HAD. WE'VE BEEN HAVING QUITE A BIT OF BLOWING DIRT EVERY YEAR SINCE THE DROUTH [DROUGHT] STARTED, NOT ONLY HERE, BUT ALL OVER THE GREAT PLAINS. MANY DAYS THIS SPRING THE AIR IS JUST FULL OF DIRT COMING, LITERALLY, FOR HUNDREDS OF MILES. IT SIFTS INTO EVERYTHING. AFTER WE WASH THE DISHES AND PUT THEM AWAY, SO MUCH DUST SIFTS INTO THE CUPBOARDS THAT WE MUST WASH THEM AGAIN BEFORE THE NEXT MEAL. CLOTHES IN THE CLOSETS ARE COVERED WITH DUST.**"**

—ANN MARIE LOW, *a North Dakota farmer's daughter in her early twenties, from her diary entry, April 25, 1934*

How did President Franklin Delano Roosevelt find jobs for 4 million Americans?

He created them. Unlike President Hoover before him, President Franklin Delano Roosevelt (often called FDR) believed that the federal government needed to step in to pull the country out of the Depression and help those who were suffering. As soon as he took office in 1933, FDR rolled up his sleeves and went to work. He didn't expect to find easy answers to the nation's problems, but he planned to try, try, and try again until he found some solutions.

FDR's first one hundred days in office were a whirlwind of activity. The president proposed dozens of new programs under a plan he called the "New Deal." Congress passed an incredible number of new laws, sometimes without even reading them. The New Deal resulted in an alphabet soup of agencies and programs that controlled business and banking and poured government money into rebuilding the economy. Some of the major New Deal acts and agencies and their duties included:

• The Securities and Exchange Commission (SEC), which regulated the stock market

- The Federal Deposit Insurance Corporation (FDIC), which insured bank deposits so people wouldn't lose their savings

- The Social Security Act, which established old-age pensions and unemployment and welfare benefits

- The Tennessee Valley Authority (TVA), which developed water power in the Tennessee River Valley

- The Civilian Conservation Corps (CCC), which put hundreds of thousands of young men to work improving national parks, planting trees, and building roads, trails, and campgrounds

- The Works Progress Administration (WPA), which created jobs for millions of Americans building highways, buildings, bridges, dams, and tunnels, and doing artistic projects from painting murals to recording oral histories

Some New Deal programs were more successful than others, but together they were almost revolutionary. The New Deal changed America forever. It expanded the federal government and made Americans dependent on it in ways that would have been unthinkable before the Depression. Economic crisis had done much to change Americans' attitudes about the responsibilities of government.

AMERICAN VOICES

❝This is pre-eminently the time to speak the truth, the whole truth, frankly and boldly. Nor need we shrink from honestly facing conditions in our country today. This great nation will endure as it has endured, will revive and will prosper.

"So first of all let me assert my firm belief that the only thing we have to fear is fear itself—nameless, unreasoning, unjustified terror which paralyzes needed efforts to convert retreat into advance.**❞**

—Franklin D. Roosevelt, *from his first inaugural address, March 4, 1933*

What was one of FDR's most important roles as president?

That of cheerleader-in-chief. FDR's New Deal did a great deal for the nation, but his optimism, heartfelt reassurance, and chin-up attitude may have done more than anything else to put America on the road to recovery. In his very first week in the White House, the president began broadcasting "fireside chats" over the radio. In these friendly speeches, FDR explained things like the banking system and the New Deal and reassured Americans that the nation would recover. He always began his chats with the words, "My friends." And indeed he did sound like a caring friend or family member who was sitting right in your living room.

Perhaps part of the reason FDR seemed so approachable was that Americans knew the president had suffered, too. In 1921 FDR had been stricken with polio, a disease that had left him paralyzed from the waist down and confined to a wheelchair (though he could stand with heavy leg braces). Struggling against the disease had made FDR's character stronger. He seemed more aware of the underdog. He changed the government accordingly, opening it to those who historically had been excluded, including blacks, Jews, Eastern Europeans, Catholics, American Indians, and women. FDR appointed the first female cabinet member, Secretary of Labor Frances Perkins.

Whom did FDR call his "eyes and ears"?

Eleanor Roosevelt visits a women's dormitory for African-American war workers.

His wife, First Lady Eleanor Roosevelt. Eleanor was an intelligent, independent woman who had almost as much energy as her uncle, Teddy Roosevelt. (FDR was related to Teddy, too—they were fifth cousins.) Eleanor didn't run around the Washington Monument at night, like Uncle Teddy, but she did work tirelessly to help the unemployed and disadvantaged, especially women, blacks, and young people. She wrote a daily newspaper column, held her own press conferences, and chaired committees. She traveled around the nation when her wheelchair-bound husband couldn't, giving speeches, visiting the poorest neighborhoods, and even inspecting the depths of coal mines to see if they were safe. (The first lady traveled so much, in fact, that a newspaper once poked fun at her with its headline, "Mrs. Roosevelt Spends Night at the White House!") Eleanor reported to FDR what she had seen and learned, and she let him know when there were things she thought he could be doing better. The well-loved Mrs. Roosevelt, a leader in her own right, became a role model for future first ladies.

She wrote in her book *You Learn by Living,* "You gain strength, courage and confidence by every experience in which you really stop to look fear in the face. You are able to say to yourself, I lived through this horror. I can take the next thing that comes along. . . . You must do the thing you think you cannot do."

Where did Americans go to forget their troubles?

To the movies. Even though the first movies were silent, by 1925 they had become America's most popular form of entertainment. After the first feature-length "talkie," *The Jazz Singer*, appeared in 1927, the demand for movies could hardly be met. Ticket prices were low enough during the Depression that about 60 percent of the population saw at least one movie a week. People spent what little money they had to escape their worries and lose themselves in the enchantment of stars like Greta Garbo, Clark Gable, the Marx Brothers, and little Shirley Temple. Glitz and glamour oozed off the big screen in the 1930s. It was the golden age of Hollywood, and studios created scenes and characters that were larger than life, even in black and white. By the end of the decade, moviegoers got the full rainbow of film effects in the first major Technicolor movies, *The Wizard of Oz* and *Gone With the Wind*.

SETTING IT STRAIGHT

Did the New Deal bring America out of the Depression?

No. The New Deal was an enormous package of programs that did put 4 million people back to work. Yet despite its best efforts, there were still 9 million Americans unemployed. It would take something even bigger to end the Depression. Unfortunately, that something was another world war.

World War II began in Europe in 1939. The United States entered the war in 1941, and by 1943 almost everyone was back to work. And no wonder: During the war, America would produce 297,000 planes, 86,000 tanks, 76,000 ships, and huge amounts of other vehicles, arms, and ammunition.

★ Roosevelt saw the nation through two of its greatest crises. He became the only president in American history to be elected to four terms. FDR had been a great president, but a few years after he died a constitutional amendment limited future presidents to serving only two full terms.

How did the First World War ignite the Second World War?

It wasn't so much the war as the peace that followed. The Treaty of Versailles had treated Germany very badly, leaving the country poor and humiliated. The worldwide depression made life in Germany even worse, and many people felt scared and directionless. Several European nations turned to powerful leaders—Adolf Hitler in Germany, Benito Mussolini in Italy, and Joseph Stalin in Russia—who ran strict totalitarian governments that promised to restore national wealth and pride.

In Germany and Italy, and also in Japan, these governments were part of a movement called *fascism*. Fascist leaders built up powerful armies to kill or intimidate those who seemed to threaten their authority. They were fiercely nationalistic, and they believed that their own races were superior to others. They believed that they had the right to trample all over weaker nations and abuse "inferior" groups, even within their own nations. Germany wanted to conquer Europe, Italy to dominate Africa, and Japan to rule over a New World Order in Asia.

Hitler youth salute their Nazi leader in Germany.

Hitler came to power in 1933 at the head of the Nazi Party. (The Nazis were the fascist party in Germany.) Within five years he was invading his neighboring countries. Hitler's goal was to reunite the German-speaking people whose land had been carved into independent countries by the Treaty of Versailles. He absorbed Austria, took Czechoslovakia, then continued on to Poland. France and Great Britain had tried to negotiate with Hitler, hoping that if they gave him part of what he wanted, he'd go home. But when he invaded Poland, which France and Britain had pledged to support, both countries declared war on Germany.

World War II had begun. France and Great Britain (and its empire, including Australia, Canada, India, and New Zealand), along with China and the United States, would eventually form the Allies. On the other side were the Axis powers of Germany, Italy, and Japan. The Soviet Union was aligned with the Axis until 1941, when Germany violated the nonaggression pact the two had signed and invaded the Soviet Union. Then the Soviets switched to the Allies.

How long did the United States mind its own business?

After the death toll of World War I, most Americans wanted no part of foreign wars. Yet some Americans, including President Roosevelt, did want to jump in and help Britain defeat Hitler, who by 1940 controlled much of Western Europe. There was little FDR could do in the face of a strongly *isolationist* (anti-foreign involvement) Congress and public, but he was able to work out a deal called Lend-Lease. This allowed the United States to loan tanks, airplanes, and ships to any country whose defense was important to America. Roosevelt compared it to lending a neighbor a garden hose to put out a fire.

Pearl Harbor naval base in blaze after attack

But on December 7, 1941, everything changed. America united behind war when Japan bombed the U.S. naval base at Pearl Harbor, Hawaii. On December 8, Congress declared war on Japan, and a few days later, Japan's allies, Germany and Italy, declared war on the United States.

World War II was truly a global war. It involved 70 million soldiers from forty countries and was fought on five continents and almost every ocean. It was the most destructive war in history, and not only because so many nations were involved. New technology enabled both sides to wage war in a more far-reaching and impersonal way than ever before—from the skies. World War II was the first war in which airplanes, and air strikes, played major roles. Each side dropped huge numbers of bombs on military targets and also on cities, killing millions of civilians. Air-raid drills and nightly blackouts (to reduce the numbers of brightly lit targets) became common. Other new techniques and technology included radar, guided missiles, vehicles that could move on land and water, jeeps, and, in the end, the deadly atomic bomb.

One of the darkest, most horrifying atrocities of the war was the Holocaust, the Nazis' mass murder of millions of Jews and other people. Hitler wanted to rule the world with a "master race" of white people he called Aryans. To make his ruling class pure, he set out to get rid of anyone who, he thought, threatened Aryan supremacy. Jews were at the top of this list. Hitler's "Final Solution" began with rounding up European Jews and imprisoning them in concentration camps, some of which were merely death factories, in Germany and Poland. By the end of the war, the Nazis had killed more than 6 million Jews. But Hitler didn't stop there. He also slaughtered Slavs, Gypsies, homosexuals, the disabled, and anyone who didn't agree with him. Nazi racism led to the murder of more than 11 million people.

Americans heard stories about what the Nazis were doing to the Jews, but mostly the news seemed too awful to believe. The United States did very little—it didn't even let in some Jews and Eastern Europeans who were fleeing the Nazis. There was racism, fear, and anti-Semitism in the United States, too.

Such books as Anne Frank's *Diary of a Young Girl* helped educate people around the world about the Holocaust. Shortly before she and her family were arrested and sent to German concentration camps, she wrote, "In spite of everything, I still believe that people are really good at heart."

Were all the World War II prison camps in Europe?

No. Unfortunately, America had its own camps during the war—Japanese internment camps. These camps were not concentration camps, but they were prisons. They were surrounded by barbed wire, and guards shot anyone who tried to run away. The government created the camps because, after the surprise bombing of Pearl Harbor, many Americans believed that Japanese Americans would help the enemy. Even though these Americans had done nothing wrong, in 1942 military guards took more than 120,000 of them to prison camps. They had been given only a few days' notice to sell their homes and other possessions before they left, which meant most were forced to accept humiliatingly low prices for their family treasures and heirlooms.

In the barren camps, Japanese Americans struggled to maintain their dignity and some kind of normal life. They planted gardens, went to school and church, played in bands, and formed baseball leagues. Most remained in the camps until the end of the war, though some were hired to pick crops because of the wartime labor shortage, or were relocated to army units. All remained loyal to the United States. One all-Japanese-American regiment that fought in Italy came out of the war with more medals than any other unit in the entire U.S. army. In 1988 Congress issued a formal apology to sixty thousand living survivors of the camps.

AMERICAN VOICES

"It [THE CAMP] WAS NOT LIKE ANYTHING THAT COULD EVEN BE CALLED CIVILIZED. ONE ROOM WITH IRON BEDS FOR EACH PERSON, NOTHING ELSE . . . NO PRIVACY, EVEN IN THE BATHROOMS. WE WERE ALLOWED JUST ONE BAG EACH THAT YOU HAD TO BE ABLE TO CARRY TO TAKE WITH YOU. WOULD YOU KNOW WHAT TO TAKE IF YOU WERE TOLD TO PACK JUST ONE BAG NOT EVEN KNOWING WHERE YOU WERE GOING AND FOR HOW LONG?"

—TERRY GRIMMESEY JANZAN, *a Japanese American who was taken to Posten internment camp in Arizona in 1942, when she was about twelve*

Who was "Rosie the Riveter"?

Rosie the Riveter was the symbol of the more than 6 million women who stepped up and took military and nonmilitary jobs while men were off fighting in World War II. She appeared as a character on a famous wartime poster, rolling up her sleeves and saying, "We Can Do It!" Rosie's real-life sisters, American women, became an essential part of the Allied victory. Staffed by women, factories that usually churned out everyday consumer goods shifted their production to round-the-clock assembly of planes, tanks, weapons, and ammunition. Some women were actually *riveting*, or firing bolts into airplane panels with a rivet gun. Others were building tanks, jeeps, or guns; delivering mail; pumping gas; or fighting fires. Women took pride in the new skills and freedom they gained working for victory and for their families. But the gains Rosie made would last only as long as the war. When men came home, women were asked to leave their jobs to make way for the returning soldiers.

It wasn't only Rosie who worked on the home front. Everyone did his or her part for the war effort. Children collected rubber and scrap metal to be turned into war equipment. Women mended their families' old clothing to make it last longer. People carpooled, kept their heat low to save fuel, and bought war bonds as a way to loan the government money. Everyone received ration stamps that allowed them to buy limited amounts of goods like butter, sugar, coffee, meat, and even leather shoes. Many families grew their own vegetables in "victory gardens" so that more of the farmers' produce could go to the troops overseas.

Who said, "Milkman, keep those bottles quiet"?

Singer Ella Mae Morse sang those words in a wartime song—a plea to let women who worked the night shift get a little morning rest. Patriotic, sentimental, and even silly songs helped lift the nation's spirits during hard times on the home front. Popular tunes included "Praise the Lord and Pass the Ammunition," "Ac-cent-tchu-ate the Positive," "Good-bye, Mama, I'm Off to Yokohama," and the fast-moving swing of "Boogie Woogie Bugle Boy" and "In the Mood."

AMERICAN ENGLISH

Like earlier wars, World War II gave American English many new words. Some had been used before but were not widely known. Others were invented during the war. These short and punchy new words included *jeep, dog tag, booby trap, walkie-talkie, bazooka, goofing off, gizmo,* and *G.I.* (originally the initials stood for Galvanized Iron garbage cans, then Government Issue, but soon came to mean soldier).

MAJOR MILESTONES IN WORLD WAR II
1938–1945

1938

MARCH 12   Hitler occupies Austria and makes it part of Germany.

SEPTEMBER 29   The Munich Pact: Britain and France allow Hitler to take over the Sudetenland, an area of Czechoslovakia with a large German-speaking population.

1939

MARCH 14   Hitler takes over the rest of Czechoslovakia.

SEPTEMBER 1   Germany invades Poland.

SEPTEMBER 3   Britain declares war on Germany; France, Australia, New Zealand, India, and Canada follow.

1940

MARCH 18   Germany and Italy announce an "Axis" alliance against Britain and France.

JUNE 14   Paris falls to the Germans.

JUNE 22   France surrenders to Germany.

JULY 10   The Battle of Britain. In the world's first major air battle, Germany begins a devastating air war over England. After four months of bombing, Britain wins in October.

NOVEMBER 5   FDR wins reelection to an unprecedented third term as president.

1941

JUNE 22   Germany invades the Soviet Union.

DECEMBER 7   Pearl Harbor. Japanese bombers attack the U.S. naval base at Pearl Harbor, Hawaii, destroying 150 planes and 19 ships on the island and killing 2,403 people.

DECEMBER 8   FDR calls December 7 "a date which will live in infamy" and asks Congress to declare war on Japan; Britain and Canada then do so as well.

DECEMBER 11   Germany and Italy declare war on the United States; China declares war on the Axis.

1942

JANUARY 2   Japan takes control of the Philippines.

JUNE 3–6   The battle of Midway. Allies win a crucial victory in the Pacific war, ending Japanese naval advantage and threats to Australia.

AUGUST 7   U.S. Marines land on Guadalcanal in the Solomon Islands, northeast of Australia. Ultimately the U.S. Marines win the island and put the Allies on a path to victory in the Pacific.

AUGUST 22   Germans begin a five-month attack on Stalingrad. After hundreds of thousands of deaths on both sides, the German attack fails, and the tide of war turns in favor of the Allies.

1943

MAY 13   All Axis troops in North Africa, more than 250,000, surrender to the Allies.

JULY 10   The Allied invasion of Italy begins.

1944

JUNE 6   D day marks the invasion of German-occupied Europe. The largest invasion force in history—5,000 ships, 11,000 airplanes, and 50,000 motorcycles, tanks, and bulldozers— lands on the Normandy coast of France (a bloody and heroic event later captured in the 1998 film *Saving Private Ryan*). After fierce fighting and heavy casualties on both sides, a million Allied troops land in Europe.

AUGUST 25   French troops retake Paris.

SEPTEMBER 3–4   Allies liberate Brussels and Antwerp, Belgium.

OCTOBER 20   U.S. General Douglas MacArthur returns to the Philippines.

NOVEMBER 7   Roosevelt wins an unprecedented fourth term as president.

DECEMBER 16   The Battle of the Bulge, Germany's last major attempt to repel the Allies, creates a bulge in the Allied lines, but Germany is ultimately defeated.

1945

FEBRUARY 4–11   Roosevelt, British Prime Minister Winston Churchill, and Soviet dictator Joseph Stalin meet in Yalta (now in Ukraine) to discuss the final attack on Germany and postwar plans for the Allies.

MARCH 16   Americans win the battle for Iwo Jima, the last
strategic island on the way to Japan, but suffer 25,000
casualties.

APRIL 12   President Roosevelt dies. The nation, and the world,
mourns; even Japan issues a sympathetic message. Vice
President Harry Truman is sworn in as president.

APRIL 30   Hitler kills himself in his bombproof bunker in
Berlin.

MAY 7   Germany surrenders.

JUNE 21   U.S. troops capture Okinawa, Japan, after three
months of bloody battle.

AUGUST 6   The United States drops the atomic bomb on
Hiroshima, Japan, killing 80,000, severely wounding another
100,000, and leveling 4.7 square miles of the city. About
120,000 will die later of radiation poisoning.

AUGUST 8   The Soviet Union declares war on Japan.

AUGUST 9   The United States drops another atomic bomb on
Nagasaki, Japan.

SEPTEMBER 2   Japan surrenders.

⭐ America's Navajo "code talkers" proved essential to victories in the
Pacific throughout the war. These U.S. Marines, who were also members
of the Navajo Nation, were assigned to every military unit in the Pacific.
There they exchanged important messages in a code the Japanese never
broke—their own language.

Did the United States have to drop the atomic bombs on Japan?

Many people have asked this question, and there isn't an easy
answer. The atomic bomb, developed during the war, was the
newest kind of deadly weapon—a nuclear one. President
Truman's advisors told him that dropping the bomb would
actually save huge numbers of American and Japanese lives

that would otherwise be lost in an invasion of Japan. They said the war could go on for years, because it was against the Japanese military code of honor to surrender.

On the other side, critics of America's action say Japan was close to surrendering when the United States dropped the bombs. It may have been the Soviets' entrance into the war against Japan, and not the bombs, that forced Japan to surrender. Some say the bombing was a show of power, not so much to Japan, but to the Soviets. Truman rightly suspected they were not to be trusted.

⭐ World War II was the deadliest, most destructive war in history. An estimated 60 million people died worldwide. United States combat casualties were almost 300,000 dead and 700,000 wounded. Many parts of Europe and Asia were completely ruined, and millions of people had no homes to return to. As for the financial cost of the war? It was more than $1,000,000,000,000 (one trillion dollars).

What did President Truman want to do with Communism?

Keep a lid on it. Truman's policy after World War II was "containment" of Communism and the Soviet influence. The Soviets took over the countries in Eastern Europe that their army had liberated from the Germans during the war, and Truman didn't want it to go any further. He pledged that the United States would help any nation threatened by Communism.

The United States began by sending $400 million to Greece and Turkey, which appeared to be the next targets for Communist takeovers. This economic assistance was part of a program called the Marshall Plan (named after Secretary of State George C. Marshall), which offered money to America's allies as well as its former enemies to help everyone recover from the war. President Truman knew his history, and he didn't want to make the same mistakes the Allies had made after World War I. He hoped that by helping both the winners and the losers, any anger, frustration, and economic troubles that might lead to Communism would be kept at bay. Sixteen Western European nations eagerly accepted relief money, and the United States handed out $13 billion between 1947 and 1951.

Was the cold war fought in Alaska?

No. (And it didn't involve any tissues or cough drops.) The cold war was a war of ideas, influence, and power between two kinds of systems: Communist dictatorship, as in the Soviet Union, and democracy and capitalism, as in the United States and Western Europe.

Nations such as England and France in Western Europe had dominated the globe for more than a century, but they were worn out after the war. The United States and the Soviet Union emerged as the two world superpowers, and the cold war was really between those two countries. Once their common enemies and need for cooperation were gone, it became more and more apparent that neither side trusted the other. "From Stettin in the Baltic to Trieste in the Adriatic," said British leader Winston Churchill in 1946, "an iron curtain has descended across the Continent." The phrase "iron curtain," meaning Soviet Communist control of Eastern Europe, became a common part of the cold war vocabulary.

It didn't help that the world had entered an age of nuclear (atomic) weapons that were capable of pulverizing entire cities. Cold war conflicts would flare up around the world for the next forty years, as each superpower sought to protect its own interests and gain allies.

After World War II, the Allies split up Germany and its capital, Berlin, and a quarter of each was occupied by the United States, Britain, France, and the Soviet Union. In 1949 the French, British, and American zones were united as the independent democracy of West Germany. The other zone became East Germany, a Communist country watched closely by the Soviets. To protect West Germany and the rest of Western Europe from possible Soviet attack, the United States, Canada, and ten European nations signed the North Atlantic Treaty, which created the North Atlantic Treaty Organization, or NATO.

West Germans peer over the Berlin Wall, which literally divided the city in 1961.

What other United group does the United States belong to?

The United Nations. During the war, the Allies began to plan for a peacekeeping body to help prevent future wars. In 1945 fifty nations, including the United States and the Soviet Union, joined the U.N. It would not be long before the strength and abilities of the U.N. were tested in the Korean War (see page 171).

CHAPTER 9

Cold Wars, Hot Wars, and Freedom Riders

"I have a dream that one day this nation will rise up and live out the true meaning of its creed: 'We hold these truths to be self-evident; that all men are created equal.'"

—THE REV. DR. MARTIN LUTHER KING, JR., *August 28, 1963*

Did Americans hunt for witches in the 1950s?

Not exactly, but they did go on "witch hunts" for suspected Communists. Americans had been worrying about the "Red Menace" of Communism for years, but after World War II suspicions reached hysterical heights. Many Americans felt the country was losing the cold war, and they decided it was because Communists in America were working for the Soviets. In response to these fears, President Truman set up loyalty boards to search out any "disloyal persons" in the federal government. No Communist spies were discovered there, but all the looking around started anti-Communist witch hunts in which thousands were accused and brought down by suspicion rather than fact.

The witch hunts were fueled by a senator from Wisconsin named Joseph McCarthy. McCarthy was looking for something to save his sinking reputation, and he decided Communism was the perfect issue. In 1950 he began accusing hundreds of people of Communist activity. McCarthy was an outrageous liar who had no evidence for his accusations, and he never proved even one case. *McCarthyism*, which has since come to mean making unfounded accusations against innocent people, destroyed reputations and ruined thousands of lives. Some of those accused were *blacklisted*—their names were put on a list of people who should not be hired for any jobs.

McCarthy was finally brought down in 1954 when he accused the entire U.S. army of being riddled with Communists. During the televised Army-McCarthy hearings, millions watched as his unfounded attacks were exposed. The army's lawyer, Joseph Welch, told McCarthy, "Until this moment, Senator, I think I never really gauged your cruelty or your recklessness. . . . Have you no decency, sir, at long last? Have you left no sense of decency?"

Why did America fight a war in Korea?

Take a wild guess . . . Communism! In the 1950s the cold war felt its first major burst of heat. It happened in the East Asian country of Korea, which had been divided at the 38th parallel after World War II. North Korea was under the Soviet sphere of influence, South Korea under the American. Free elections

A South Korean flag waves in the foreground as U.S. cavalry troopers head toward the 38th parallel.

were supposed to reunite the country after the war, but the Communists never let that happen. North Korea's leader, Kim Il Sung, planned to make all of Korea Communist. His well-prepared army, armed and trained by the Soviets, invaded South Korea in June 1950. The United Nations, led by the United States, sent soldiers to help South Korea. This was a test for the world, and for President Truman, who didn't want to appear weak in the stand against Communism.

At first the U.S. army did poorly, but then it started to win. It pushed the North Koreans back to the border at the 38th parallel. United Nations forces continued to push the North Koreans back until they were nearly at the Chinese border. Big mistake. This brought China's well-trained, well-equipped, and large army into the war, pushing the U.N. forces back to the 38th parallel. For two more years the battles raged back and forth, neither side gaining significant ground. Meanwhile MacArthur defied Truman's orders to keep the war limited to Korea and made open threats against China. In April of 1951 Truman removed him from command.

In 1953 a cease-fire ended the conflict at the 38th parallel, the same place it was begun. The United States had never officially declared war, and no one had won. But Americans had proved that they'd stand up to Communism. The cost was 54,000 Americans, several thousand other U.N. soldiers, and more than 1 million Koreans dead. Today Korea remains divided, despite attempts in 1999 to begin rebuilding a unified nation.

★ In 1950, the same year the Korean conflict started, President Truman sent aid to France, which was fighting Communist rebels in the Southeast Asian country of Vietnam. France had ruled Vietnam and its neighbors Laos and Cambodia before Japan invaded during World War II. Now France wanted its colonies back. But a Communist leader in Vietnam, Ho Chi Minh, wanted his country to be independent. France asked the United States for help fighting these Viet Minh rebels, so the United States sent military advisors, supplies, and millions of dollars. Over the next twenty years, the Vietnam conflict would pull the United States in deeper and deeper, like a pool of quicksand.

In the 1950s, America saw a boom in:

a) babies

b) houses and cars

c) fast-food restaurants

d) television sets

e) popular music

f) all of the above

The answer is *f*. What people think of as the culture of the 1950s actually started in 1945, with the end of World War II. The soldiers came home and wanted to settle into a quiet, normal, comfortable life. Many went to school on the G.I. Bill, which gave veterans a free college education, or took up the jobs they had left behind. Soldiers got married and needed affordable housing, and American suburbs spread out in waves of small, look-alike houses to meet the demand. Builder William Levitt applied the assembly line method to house building in Levittown, Long Island. Soon his crews were putting up thirty-six homes a day!

Those homes were soon filled with diapers and bottles; more than 76.4 million "baby boomers" were born between 1946 and

1964. And the driveways were filled with cars, since a home in the suburbs meant a commute to work in the city. More cars meant drive-in movies, drive-in restaurants, and the first Holiday Inn. The war had set the stage for a boom in both making and buying goods, and factories that had been making war materials around the clock turned to making cars, TVs, refrigerators, dishwashers, bicycles, and other goodies.

But postwar prosperity and life in the suburbs were almost exclusively for whites. Most blacks remained in the cities, where one-third of them barely earned enough to live on (compared with the one-eighth of whites in this situation). Blacks soldiers had served honorably during the war but returned home to find conditions were no better than they'd been before.

What started by the roadside and spread around the world?

A certain restaurant sporting golden arches. In the 1940s two brothers named Dick and Maurice McDonald opened a roadside hamburger stand in San Bernardino, California. Their burgers, kept warm by infrared lamps, and their speedy and reliable service caught the eye of a traveling salesman of milkshake machines. The salesman, Ray Kroc, liked what he saw. He talked the McDonalds into selling him the rights to their name and methods—and thus the McDonald's franchise restaurants were born.

In 1955 Kroc opened the first McDonald's franchise restaurant in Des Plaines, Illinois. On the menu: hamburgers, cheeseburgers, french fries, soft drinks, milk shakes, coffee, and milk. The restaurant made $366.12 that first day. The success of the McDonald's formula—inexpensive, predictable food, delivered quickly in a clean environment—led to a national boom in fast-food restaurants. Today the golden arches are a familiar sight in most countries, marking thirty thousand restaurants around the world.

GREAT AMERICAN PASTIMES

What was the new living room fixture of the 1950s?

Here's a hint: In 1939, when this item was demonstrated at the New York World's Fair, *The New York Times* said it would never seriously compete with radio because "people must sit and keep their eyes glued on a screen; the average American family hasn't the time for it." Can you guess what it is? Television! TV had been around since the late 1930s, but it really took off in the fifties. More than 4 million TV sets were sold in 1950—that's 78,000 a week. By 1960, 90 percent of homes had a TV, and the new medium was changing the nation. Families talked less and watched more. They saw commercials that created a desire for things they hadn't even known they wanted. Perhaps most importantly, television gave Americans more of a common culture. Across the country, people could watch the same quiz shows, soap operas, variety shows, westerns, professional sports, news events, and situation-comedies such as *Leave It to Beaver* and *I Love Lucy*.

In the 1950s young America found a king—the King of Rock 'n' Roll. His name was Elvis Presley. Elvis didn't invent rock 'n' roll, which combined traditionally black rhythm and blues music with white country and western, but he was its first big superstar. (Other rock 'n' rollers who helped shape the infectious music include Chuck Berry, Little Richard, and Buddy Holly.) Elvis's fans were wild for him. Between 1956 and 1958, he made fourteen records that each sold at least a million copies. Many adults didn't approve of his music or the way he moved his hips when he sang, but this only made rebellious youths—now called teenagers—love him more. If you've heard "Hound Dog" or "Jailhouse Rock," you know why it's hard to resist him.

How did a third-grade girl in Kansas change history?

She and her family challenged the bad old idea of "separate but equal." In the South and in some parts of the North, segregated schools, hotels, restaurants, water fountains, rest rooms, and other places were common. "Separate but equal" had been the way of life for more than a half-century, since the Supreme Court made the practice legal in *Plessy* v. *Ferguson* (see page 128) in 1896. But it was plain to see that separate wasn't equal at all. This reality was especially glaring in public schools, particularly in the South. Southern schools for whites were new, well equipped, and adequately staffed. Schools for blacks were often one-room shacks without running water, run by a single teacher.

So if you were Reverend Oliver Brown of Topeka, Kansas, you might try to enroll your daughter Linda in third grade at the all-white school just four blocks from your house—rather than in the run-down all-black school, which was all the way across town. When Oliver Brown did just that in 1951, authorities at the white school told him he couldn't. Brown turned around and sued the school board of Topeka. Similar lawsuits were brought in four other states, and each was taken all the way to the Supreme Court. There, all five were tried together in 1953 as *Brown* v. *Board of Education of Topeka, Kansas*. (Brown's name was listed because it came first alphabetically in the list of lawsuits brought against the states.)

The NAACP represented the children in court, and representing the NAACP was a superb lawyer named Thurgood Marshall. (Fourteen years later, Marshall would become the first black Supreme Court justice.) The justices were split in their opinions until the Court's chief justice Fred Vinson died in 1954 and was replaced by Earl Warren. Warren knew it was essential for the Court to issue a unanimous decision in *Brown* because it was such an important, landmark case. He quietly persuaded all the justices to his side, finally writing the Court's 9–0 decision that "Separate educational facilities are inherently unequal."

But the decision was only the beginning. It still had to be enforced. The Court hadn't said how desegregation should be achieved, only that it must be done with "all deliberate speed." To some states, that meant never. Many school systems would take their own sweet time.

AMERICAN VOICES

"WE COME THEN TO THE QUESTION PRESENTED: DOES SEGREGATION OF CHILDREN IN PUBLIC SCHOOLS SOLELY ON THE BASIS OF RACE, EVEN THOUGH THE PHYSICAL FACILITIES AND OTHER 'TANGIBLE' FACTORS MAY BE EQUAL, DEPRIVE THE CHILDREN OF THE MINORITY GROUP OF EQUAL EDUCATIONAL OPPORTUNITIES? WE BELIEVE THAT IT DOES. . . .

"TO SEPARATE THEM FROM OTHERS OF SIMILAR AGE AND QUALIFICATIONS SOLELY BECAUSE OF THEIR RACE GENERATES A FEELING OF INFERIORITY AS TO THEIR STATUS IN THE COMMUNITY THAT MAY AFFECT THEIR HEARTS AND MINDS IN A WAY UNLIKELY EVER TO BE UNDONE. . . .

"WE CONCLUDE THAT IN THE FIELD OF PUBLIC EDUCATION THE DOCTRINE OF 'SEPARATE BUT EQUAL' HAS NO PLACE. SEPARATE EDUCATIONAL FACILITIES ARE INHERENTLY UNEQUAL."

—CHIEF JUSTICE EARL WARREN, *from the unanimous opinion in Brown v. Board of Education of Topeka, Kansas, May 17, 1954*

Were public schools the only places being integrated?

No. In the years before *Brown* v. *Board of Education*, other American institutions slowly began to integrate. One was the military. People saw how unfair it was that black soldiers who had fought bravely in World War II were denied basic human rights at home. So in 1948 President Truman ordered the military to begin desegregating.

The year before, major league baseball took the first step toward integration when the Brooklyn Dodgers hired a talented athlete from the Negro leagues, first baseman Jackie Robinson. Dodgers general manager Branch Rickey wanted Robinson on his team. Rickey knew how tough it would be to break the color barrier, but he knew Jackie was strong enough, and good enough, to do it. During that first season, Jackie held his head high while he endured racist jeers, spitting "fans," and even death threats. But he remained a gentleman through it all, and he played fabulous baseball. He was named Rookie of the Year and helped his team win the National League pennant. Jackie Robinson gained the respect of blacks and whites alike, paving the way for blacks in baseball, and in sports in general.

Where did Rosa Parks park herself, in protest?

Rosa Parks was a forty-two-year-old seamstress in Montgomery, Alabama, an active member of the Montgomery chapter of the NAACP, and a respected member of the community. After a long day at work on December 1, 1955, Parks boarded the city bus to go home. Buses in the South were segregated: Whites sat in the front, blacks in the back. The seats in the middle were up for grabs, but blacks could only sit in them if there were enough seats for whites. Rosa Parks sat in the middle of the bus, and when the seats around her began filling up with white passengers, the driver shouted for her to give up her seat. But Rosa Parks was tired. Tired from working all day, and tired of being pushed around. She stayed right where she was. The police soon arrived and arrested her.

The news of Parks's arrest spread like wildfire through Montgomery's black community. The city's black leaders had been looking for someone to test the segregation of the bus system, and they quickly decided respectable Parks was the one to do it. Quickly after Parks's arrest, the leaders organized a boycott of the city buses, urging blacks to use other forms of transportation. For more than a year, through all kinds of weather and even more kinds of abuse, the city's black citizens carpooled or walked to work and school.

Some boycotters went to jail or had their houses burned and churches bombed, but that didn't stop them.

The leader of the Montgomery bus boycott was a twenty-six-year-old minister named Martin Luther King, Jr. The Rev. Dr. King urged peaceful resistance against injustice, and his tactics paid off. In 1956 the Supreme Court ordered Montgomery's buses desegregated. The victory was just the beginning, since it only applied to buses in Montgomery. For the next ten years, nonviolent protests marked the *civil rights movement*, or the fight by blacks and their supporters to end segregation and gain equal rights. Many of the protests were led by King and the Southern Christian Leadership Conference (SCLC), which he helped found in 1957 to fight segregation.

AMERICAN VOICES

❝THE ONLY TIRED I WAS, WAS TIRED OF GIVING IN.❞

—ROSA PARKS

What inspired Dr. King's methods of nonviolent protest?

Dr. Martin Luther King, Jr., was the son of a minister and a well-educated minister himself. When he was in school studying religion, King learned about Mohandas (Mahatma) Gandhi, who developed the concept of nonviolent protest in India and used it to win his country's independence from Britain in 1947. King was inspired by the virtue and dignity of Gandhi 's techniques and combined them with the foundations of Christianity—love, faith, humility, hope, forgiveness, compassion—as the weapons of his resistance against segregation and racial hatred. Dr. King and his followers trained blacks to summon all their courage and self-control and restrain their anger. In workshops throughout the South, participants had to sit quietly while others, pretending to be racists, hurled insults and threats, and even spit at them.

Were the Little Rock Nine a rock 'n' roll band?

No, they were a group of nine black students who were the first to integrate an all-white high school in Little Rock, Arkansas, in 1957. Three years after *Brown* v. *Board of Education* had said that desegregation should proceed with "all deliberate speed," there still were no classrooms in the deep South that were integrated.

In 1957 a federal judge ordered white schools in Little Rock to allow black students to attend. When the nine black students arrived on the first day of school, they thought the 270 members of the Arkansas National Guard posted outside the school were there to protect them. But Arkansas governor Orval Faubus had ordered the troops to *stop* the nine students from entering the school. On national television and around the world, viewers watched as the guards let an angry, jeering mob spit at and curse at the teenagers. President Eisenhower finally had to send 1,100 army troops to Little Rock to protect the nine students. The troops stayed in the school for the rest of the school year. Despite the taunting, name-calling, tripping, kicking, and other abuse the Little Rock Nine suffered, they held their heads high and stuck it out.

What were civil rights activists up to in the early 1960s?

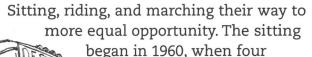

Sitting, riding, and marching their way to more equal opportunity. The sitting began in 1960, when four black college freshmen in Greensboro, North Carolina, sat down and quietly asked for service at an all-white Woolworth's lunch counter. The freshmen had food poured on their heads, were shoved off their stools, and were arrested. But their actions sparked a wave of sit-ins in more than one hundred cities. By the end of the year, after some 50,000 other people had protested and 3,600 of them been arrested, lunch counters were opened to blacks in Greensboro and many other places.

Around the same time, a civil rights group, the Congress of Racial Equality (CORE), organized "Freedom Rides," in which blacks and whites rode together through the southern states refusing to obey the segregation rules on the buses or in the stations. Violence broke out against the people on the buses, but the freedom riders would not give up. Eventually federal marshals were sent to protect them.

In 1963 more violence erupted when Martin Luther King, Jr., decided to take segregation protests to Birmingham, Alabama, "the most segregated city in the United States." Thousands of peaceful protesters marched to integrate downtown stores, only to be met with policemen's billy clubs, dogs, tear gas, and painful spray from high-powered fire hoses. So many demonstrators were thrown in jail that civil rights leaders asked child volunteers to continue the protests. Hundreds of brave children marched and met the same fate as the adults. People across the country and around the world watched these events on television, and they were outraged. Police brutality did the exact opposite of what it was supposed to: Instead of stopping the protesters, it gained them sympathy and support.

The horror in Birmingham prompted President John F. Kennedy to support a national Civil Rights Act banning segregation in public facilities. To encourage passage of the bill, Dr. King and others organized a march on Washington. The event drew 250,000 blacks and whites from all over the country. It was the largest political gathering for human rights in American history. At the end of the day, Dr. King stood on the steps of the Lincoln Memorial—one hundred years after Lincoln issued the Emancipation Proclamation—and gave his famous "I Have a Dream" speech. The Civil Rights Act was passed in July 1964.

AMERICAN VOICES

"I HAVE A DREAM THAT MY FOUR CHILDREN WILL ONE DAY LIVE IN A NATION WHERE THEY WILL NOT BE JUDGED BY THE COLOR OF THEIR SKIN BUT BY THE CONTENT OF THEIR CHARACTER.**"**

—THE REV. DR. MARTIN LUTHER KING, JR., *"I Have a Dream" speech, Washington, D.C., August 28, 1963*

Did a handsome face win the presidency for John F. Kennedy?

No, but Kennedy's all-American good looks probably didn't hurt him, either. In 1960 voters crowded around their TVs to watch the first nationally televised presidential debates in American history. When Vice President Richard Nixon and Massachusetts Senator John F. Kennedy squared off, Nixon was recovering from two weeks in the hospital. He was underweight, pale, uncomfortable, and sweating under the hot lights on the set. Kennedy, on the other hand, was tan, handsome, and brimming with youthful energy. Radio listeners didn't think there was a clear winner, but television viewers were captivated by Kennedy.

The debates were not the only factor in the close election, but after Kennedy won, many people thought it was partly due to how "presidential" he had looked on television. John F. Kennedy (often called JFK) became, at forty-three years of age, the youngest president elected to office. (Teddy Roosevelt was an even younger president, but you remember that he wasn't elected.) At his inauguration, Kennedy spoke of the torch being passed to a new generation of Americans who were ready to work for human rights around the world. "Ask not what your country can do for you," he said, "ask what you can do for your country."

★ One way JFK inspired America's youths to work for their country was by creating the Peace Corps, an organization that sent American volunteers to less developed countries to make people's lives better (and to encourage American, rather than Communist, ways). College students jumped at the chance to serve. By 1963 about five thousand Peace Corps volunteers were busy teaching and working in more than forty countries.

AMERICAN ENGLISH

Many young Americans joined the Peace Corps. Others marched with Martin Luther King, Jr. And some, in their spare time—went surfing, dude. Surfer slang that entered the American vocabulary in the 1960s included *surf's up, hang ten, wipeout, stoked,* and *dude* (an older word that gained a new, all-purpose meaning of "guy").

Where did President Kennedy want to send some Americans?

To the moon. In 1957 the Soviet Union had struck a blow at American self-confidence by launching *Sputnik*, the world's first artificial satellite, into space. *Sputnik*, a little machine just larger than a basketball, orbited some 560 miles above Earth, emitting a *beep-beep-beep* radio signal and putting Americans into a tizzy. If America was the greatest nation in the world, people asked themselves, how did the Soviets beat the United States into space? And if the Soviets, a cold war competitor, could launch something like this, could they also launch

nuclear bombs? Americans realized they were behind in space science, and that was both humbling and scary.

The U.S. government, already competing with the Soviet Union to see who could build the best weapons, immediately began pouring billions of dollars into defense spending and the "space race." President Eisenhower had established the National Aeronautics and Space Administration (NASA) in 1958, and though the Soviets kept their early lead and sent the first human into space in 1961, the United States was closing the gap. The greatest feat would be to land a man on the moon, which President Kennedy pledged to do before 1970. Do you know who first walked on the moon in 1969? (See page 197.)

Why did America fear a small island in the Caribbean?

Soon after President Kennedy came into office, he learned that the Central Intelligence Agency (CIA) was planning to invade Cuba, an island just ninety miles from the southern tip of Florida. In 1958 Cuban rebels led by Fidel Castro had taken over the country. Though at first Castro was friendly to the United States, within months he had become a harsh Communist dictator with ties to the Soviet Union. The fact that Cuba was so close to the United States gave America the jitters.

Many Cubans who felt betrayed by Castro had fled to the United States (and some, such as the boy Elián Gonzalez in 1999, continue to cause great controversy). By 1961 the CIA had trained and armed fifteen hundred of them to land at Cuba's Bay of Pigs and start an uprising that would overthrow Castro. But the whole thing was poorly planned, and nothing went right. There was no uprising. More than a hundred of the invaders were killed, and more than a thousand were captured. America looked just plain foolish.

President Kennedy took all the blame himself. For this his popularity soared at home. But abroad—most importantly in the Soviet Union—he was seen as a weakling. Soviet leader Nikita Khrushchev took advantage of this apparent weakness and put nuclear missiles in Cuba in 1962. These missiles, aimed at major American cities and military bases, were spotted by American spy planes flying over Cuba. What should President Kennedy do? If he invaded or pushed the Soviets too far, it could be World War III—a nuclear war. Both the Americans and the Soviets had weapons that could devastate the world. President Kennedy demanded that the missile sites be taken apart and removed. (To ease tensions, he went ahead with the planned removal of U.S. missiles from Turkey, where they were threatening Russia.) In case Khrushchev didn't go along with this, Kennedy also readied the armed forces for an invasion of Cuba.

For thirteen nail-biting days in October of 1962, the world waited. Then the Soviets agreed to bring the weapons home. The Cuban Missile Crisis was over.

What was "the problem without a name"?

It was the issue discussed by author Betty Friedan in her 1963 book *The Feminine Mystique*. Friedan was a college-educated housewife and freelance writer living out the 1950s dream of suburban marriage and motherhood. When she decided to write an article on suburban women, she found that many of the women she talked to were unhappy, yet they didn't know why. Friedan's article turned into *The Feminine Mystique*, which said that women's magazines, ads for new household gadgets, and TV shows like *Leave It to Beaver* and *Father Knows Best* idealized the happy housewife who devoted herself to her family and brainwashed women into thinking they were happy. She said the mass media stifled women's ambitions and shaped their attitudes about their roles in society. Deep down, she felt, many women wanted more.

Of course, not every suburban housewife felt this way. But Friedan's book got women thinking. In 1960, 36 percent of women were working for paid wages. Yet they were making much less money than men, and they were still largely confined to traditional "female" jobs like teaching or nursing. Friedan made women think again about their place in society. Her book, along with the civil rights movement, helped jump-start the modern women's movement, which would call for equal rights, equal pay, and equal respect for women.

In 1966 three hundred women founded the National Organization for Women (NOW), with Friedan as president. The organization became the largest women's rights group in American history. Its members fought for equal job and schooling opportunities, worked to get more women elected to political office, and helped win abortion rights.

Who killed JFK?

On November 22, 1963, President Kennedy and his wife, Jackie, were in Dallas, Texas, trying to smooth relations with southern Democrats. The couple was riding down the street in a convertible when shots rang out from a nearby warehouse. Bullets struck the young president in the head, and he died soon afterward. Two days later the grief-stricken nation watched on live television as the prime suspect in the assassination, Lee Harvey Oswald, was himself shot by a nightclub owner named Jack Ruby.

After the assassination, many people did not believe that Oswald acted alone. Vice President Lyndon Baines Johnson (often called LBJ), who became president just after Kennedy died, had Chief Justice Earl Warren lead an investigation into the murder. Even though the Warren Commission concluded that Oswald did act alone and not at the behest of Communists, gangsters, white supremacists, or any other group, there are many people who still believe others were involved. However, there is no convincing evidence of a wider conspiracy.

Rachel Carson

Rachel Carson speaks to the Senate about the dangers of pesticide sprays.

Rachel Carson (1907–1964) was a biologist and author whose work sent a warning to the world: If we do not take better care of the earth, we could harm it beyond repair. Carson's research and writing about the deadly effects of pesticides like DDT helped launch the modern environmental movement.

From her early days growing up in Pennsylvania, Carson was an ardent nature lover who also liked to write. After earning a master's degree in zoology at Johns Hopkins University in 1932, Carson worked as an aquatic biologist for the U.S. Bureau of Fisheries. She became editor in chief at the U.S. Fish and Wildlife Service in 1947, devoting her extra time to writing books. Her first book, *The Sea Around Us*, became a bestseller that was translated into thirty-two languages. Two subsequent books about the sea increased Carson's fame and popularity. But it was her 1962 book, *Silent Spring*, that changed the world.

Farmers had made widespread use of pesticides to kill crop-eating insects since the 1940s. Though the pesticides were supposedly safe, *Silent Spring* told a different story. Carson's research revealed that the chemicals were actually toxic to the earth and its creatures. *Silent Spring* caused an uproar in the chemical industry. It also led the government to re-examine its policies on pesticide use. Carson testified before Congress before she died in 1964, hoping that her work would help prevent a silent spring— one where all the living things were gone.

In 1970 the United states celebrated the first Earth Day, an annual event that raises environmental awareness and encourages recycling and other programs to clean up the planet. Earth Day inspired Congress to pass the Clean Air Act and vote to create the Environmental Protection Agency.

What two wars did President Lyndon Baines Johnson wage?

After serving out Kennedy's term as president, LBJ was elected in his own right in 1964. And with that he launched an enormous program of social reform he called the "Great Society." The program was even more ambitious than FDR's New Deal.

As part of the Great Society, the president declared a war on poverty. LBJ knew what it was like to be poor—he had grown up in an impoverished part of Texas—and his goal was to rid America of poverty altogether. He created the Job Corps to train people to work and help them find jobs. He also set up Operation Head Start to help small children get ready for kindergarten, Upward Bound to help needy kids go to college, Medicare and Medicaid to help Americans pay their medical bills, and programs to protect and beautify the environment.

LBJ's Great Society did many good things. But it, and the war on poverty, were overwhelmed by Johnson's increasing commitment to another war—the war in Vietnam. Soon we were spending more money on Vietnam than on all the Great Society programs combined.

What was the "domino effect"?

According to President Eisenhower, it was the reason the United States was involved in Vietnam. If Vietnam became Communist, Eisenhower said, all of Southeast Asia might follow like a row of toppling dominoes.

In 1954 the French army had been so badly beaten by the Vietnamese that France decided to pack up its troops and go home. The peace negotiations that followed split Vietnam into North and South. They also called for an election to decide whether the two Vietnams should unite. The election was never held. France was out of the picture, but the United States stuck around. Ho Chi Minh, the president of North Vietnam, still wanted Vietnam united and independent. He had fought the French as he tried to reach this goal, and now he would

A training lecture for Vietnamese civil guard troops in Song Mao

fight the Americans. We sent money—more and more of it—directly to South Vietnam, along with troops, or "advisors." President Kennedy sent advisors, and LBJ sent more.

It was under President Johnson that U.S. troops really got into combat in Vietnam. It began in 1964 when North Vietnamese patrol ships fired on an American ship keeping watch on the Tonkin Gulf, off the shores of North Vietnam. LBJ said the ship was attacked again two days later (which turned out to be false), and that alarmed Congress enough that they passed a bill called the Gulf of Tonkin Resolution. The resolution gave the president authority to respond to this attack. We began bombing North Vietnam and sending more and more troops: In 1965 there were 75,000 Americans in Vietnam; in 1966 there were 375,000; and by 1968, 500,000. We kept fighting the Communists, and the Communists kept winning. The war seemed hopeless, but no one seemed to know how to get out.

What got longer and what got shorter during the sixties?

Teenage boys' hair got longer and teenage girls' skirts got shorter—much to the outrage of many parents. The sixties were a time of change, and that turmoil was reflected in the lives and styles of young people. Rock 'n' roll music took on a new sound and a new power when British bands such as the Beatles and the Rolling Stones became wildly popular in the United States. Fashions became shorter, brighter, and wackier, with women sporting tiny miniskirts and both sexes wearing beaded necklaces and flowered shirts.

But the counterculture movement was not only about style. It had substance, too. Young people—and many of their parents—became increasingly concerned about civil rights problems at home and the Vietnam War abroad. An increasing number of them took to the streets in protest marches.

66 Whoever heard of a revolution where they lock arms . . . singing 'we shall overcome'? You don't do that in a revolution! You don't do any singing because you're too busy swinging! 99

—Malcolm X, *1963*

Did passage of the Civil Rights Act end the civil rights movement?

No; there was still much to be done. In 1964 LBJ helped pass the Civil Rights Act, which banned discrimination in public places and in hiring and union membership. But voting rights were still a problem. Some southern states used state laws and intimidation to keep blacks from casting ballots. To draw national attention to the campaign for voting rights, in 1965 Dr. Martin Luther King, Jr., organized a fifty-eight-mile march from Selma to Montgomery, Alabama. Angry white mobs and state troopers attacked the peaceful marchers with billy clubs and tear gas. Americans watching the events on national television were outraged. So was President Johnson. He sent a Voting Rights Act to Congress, and the bill passed that year.

By the 1960s the civil rights movement was split between those who supported King's nonviolent ideas and those who'd lost patience with them and called for more aggressive ways of seeking progress. One of the early spokesmen for this movement was Malcolm X, a former criminal who had turned his life around by joining a religious group called the Nation of Islam. Malcolm said white people were devils and that blacks should separate from whites completely. Instead of using nonviolent methods, Malcolm said, blacks should fight discrimination "by any means necessary."

Civil rights activist Malcolm X

In 1964 Malcolm split from the Nation of Islam. He began to think that blacks must look within their own community for the means to achieve freedom and respect. He advocated racial equality and pride in black heritage and culture. Just as Malcolm X was changing his ideas about hatred and violence, he was killed by Black Muslims while making a speech in Harlem in 1965.

⭐ Though Malcolm X and Martin Luther King, Jr., had many of the same goals, King continued to believe in change through peaceful resistance. King began protesting the Vietnam War because he believed that the huge amounts of money being spent on the war could be put to better use at home. As he was preparing for a "poor people's march" on Washington in 1968, Dr. Martin Luther King, Jr., was assassinated in Memphis, Tennessee. In a sad reaction to his peaceful ways, violent riots broke out in 130 cities in the wake of his death.

Did other minority groups use nonviolent protest to fight for their rights?

Yes. In 1965 a Mexican-American named Cesar Chavez formed a union called the Farm Workers Association (later renamed United Farm Workers, or UFW) to fight for better wages and conditions for migrant workers. These workers, who were usually of Mexican heritage, traveled from field to field, hoping to find work. They lived in shacks or tents without heat or running water. They worked for long hours doing backbreaking jobs in unsafe conditions, all for low pay. Chavez, inspired by Mohandas Gandhi and Martin Luther King, Jr., led union members in a nonviolent strike against California grape growers to force the growers to meet the union's demands. He then led a three-hundred-mile walk across California to call attention to his cause and fasted for almost a month. Millions of Americans became aware of Chavez's cause and boycotted grapes. Eventually most of the major California grape growers agreed to sign contracts with the UFW.

GREAT AMERICAN PASTIMES

What super event took place in 1967?

The first Super Bowl, the championship game of the National Football League. In Super Bowl I, the Green Bay Packers beat the Kansas City Chiefs, 35–10, in Los Angeles.

The rules of modern American football, which developed from rugby, were first written in 1876. The association that became the National Football League was founded in 1920, when sports became more popular after World War I. But it wasn't until after World War II, when television and televised games appeared, that football really took off. Today more people watch the Super Bowl than any other televised sports event of the year.

CHAPTER 10

An American Century Ends. . . . Another Begins

"We are of course a nation of differences. Those differences don't make us weak. They're the source of our strength. . . . The question is not when we came here . . . but why our families came here. And what we did after we arrived."

—JIMMY CARTER, *1976*

What did hawks and doves have to do with the Vietnam War?

University students protest with a poster and mock casket.

"Hawks" were people who supported the war; "doves" were those who wanted peace. Vietnam was the most unpopular and divisive war in American history, and the number of doves grew as the war dragged on.

Antiwar protests started at colleges and universities and soon spread across the country. Most Americans supported LBJ and the war until the North Vietnamese led a 1968 attack called the Tet Offensive. Tet was the largest Vietnamese assault of the war, and though we pushed the North

Vietnamese back, it showed Americans that—despite what some U.S. generals had been telling them—the end of the war was not just around the corner. Protesters chanted, "Hey, hey, LBJ, how many kids did you kill today?" Under increasing attack, President Johnson decided not to run for a second full term as president and retired in January of 1969. By that year, nearly thirty-four thousand men had refused to be drafted into the army. Some turned in or burned their draft cards. Others moved to Canada to avoid the draft.

Tension mounted when four college students in an antiwar demonstration were killed by national guardsmen at Kent State University in Ohio in 1970. The following year, *The New York Times* published articles revealing that the government had deceived the American people for years about the country's increasing involvement in Vietnam and surrounding countries. These "Pentagon Papers" gave the antiwar movement new credibility, and protests grew in number until President Nixon agreed to bring U.S. troops home. The day after the last U.S. forces left Vietnam in 1975, Communist forces finished taking over the country.

MAJOR MILESTONES IN THE VIETNAM WAR 1955–1975

1955

The United States provides military training and more than $200 million in aid directly to the anti-Communist, South Vietnam government.

1961

President Kennedy sends more equipment and advisors to Vietnam; by the end of the year, there are 3,205 U.S. military personnel there.

1964

U.S. planes bomb North Vietnam in retaliation for attacks on U.S. ships; the Gulf of Tonkin Resolution gives President Johnson the power to wage war.

The war escalates when U.S. air raids begin sustained bombing of North Vietnam and the U.S. combat troops reach 125,000.

1968

The Tet Offensive shows the United States that the North Vietnamese army will be hard to defeat. American citizens increasingly turn against the war; peace talks between the United States and North Vietnam begin in Paris.

1969

President Nixon orders the secret bombing of Cambodia.

Nixon begins withdrawing U.S. troops.

1970

Four students are killed when national guardsmen open fire at an antiwar protest at Kent State University.

1971

The New York Times begins publication of the "Pentagon Papers," the top-secret history of American involvement in Vietnam.

1973

A cease-fire agreement is announced; American prisoners of war are released.

1975

North Vietnamese troops attack major South Vietnamese cities, including the capital, Saigon, causing the last Americans to flee; the South falls to the Communists the next day.

Who were the "hippies"?

Some of those who opposed the war were people who "dropped out" of mainstream society in the 1960s. These people called themselves hippies (Why? Because they were hip!), and they believed in a peaceful world where everyone loved one another. Most hippies were middle class and around college age, and their lifestyle was an escape from and rebellion against that of their parents and the older, more straight-laced generations.

There were very few true hippies, who completely dropped out of society at the time. But there was a much larger generation of young Americans who opposed the Vietnam War, worked for civil rights, and believed in more women's rights. Many of them sported long hair and worn-out blue jeans. They listened and danced to the music of Bob Dylan, Joan Baez, the Beatles, and Jimi Hendrix. Many of them took drugs, and some of them died from them. Though the hippies and other protesters of that era grew older and became more conventional, it was still a generation that helped end America's war in Vietnam and profoundly changed American culture.

Did the cold war ever thaw?

It did, but it took a long time. The thaw began with President Nixon, who visited two major Communist powers—China and the Soviet Union—in 1972. The Vietnam War had shown Nixon that something had to change between the United States and Communist countries, and his trip to Asia marked a shift in American foreign policy. It showed America that Communist powers weren't necessarily connected to one another or opposed to Western democracies.

Nixon put America on the road to full diplomatic relations with China and began *détente*, or the lessening of tension, with the Soviet Union. We began to develop friendlier relations with the Soviets and agreed to several treaties that would reduce the number of nuclear weapons. Between 1972 and 1979, Strategic Arms Limitation Talks (SALT I and II) resulted in agreements that limited each country's nuclear weapons. In 1987 President Ronald Reagan made another major breakthrough in the arms race when he and Soviet leader Mikhail Gorbachev signed the

Intermediate-Range Nuclear Forces agreement, by which each side agreed to get rid of an entire class of missiles.

66 THAT'S ONE SMALL STEP FOR MAN, ONE GIANT LEAP FOR MANKIND. 99

—*American astronaut* NEIL ARMSTRONG, *who made history on July 20, 1969, when he became the first person to set foot on the moon*

In July of 1969 people around the world saw something on television that many believed they would never see: a man walking on the moon—240,000 miles away. Some people have called the moon landing the greatest scientific accomplishment of the modern world.

Neil Armstrong's footprint on the moon marked a grand achievement in the space race.

Armstrong and fellow astronaut Buzz Aldrin spent twenty-one hours, thirty-six minutes, and twenty-one seconds on the moon. They took pictures, set up scientific experiments, collected rock samples for scientists to study back on Earth, talked to President Richard Nixon via radio, and put up an American flag and a plaque that read, "Here Men from the Planet Earth/First Set Foot upon the Moon/July 1969 AD/We Came in Peace for All Mankind."

In 1975 Americans and Soviets began to work together in space. The former rivals launched two spacecraft that docked in space for two days. The astronauts shook hands on live TV and conducted experiments together.

Why did President Nixon give up his job?

a) Congress was about to kick him out.

b) Americans found out he had CREEPs working for him.

c) He was tired of being president.

The answer is mostly letter *a*, with a little of letter *b* thrown in for good measure. Richard Nixon did some great things for the country by starting to make friends with China and the Soviet Union. But he also betrayed the nation in many ways. The criminal, secretive side of President Nixon was revealed in a scandal called "Watergate."

The Watergate crisis began to unfold when five of Nixon's staff members, who belonged to the Committee to Re-Elect the President (which became known as CREEP), were caught breaking in to the Democratic Party headquarters at the Watergate office building in Washington, D.C., in 1972. When word got out that the burglars had connections to the White House, Nixon's advisors offered to pay the burglars to keep quiet and cover up the crime. But the scandal didn't stay covered for long. Two young reporters from *The Washington Post*, Bob Woodward and Carl Bernstein, traced the crime back to the White House. The *Post* published what Woodward and Bernstein found (and in doing so acted as the watchdog the

press is supposed to be in a democratic society). A criminal investigation followed.

Nixon repeatedly denied any involvement in the Watergate burglaries or in the other illegal actions the investigations revealed (among them, that he let his staff lie, steal confidential records, and tap phones; and that he used government money to improve his homes and weaseled out of income tax payments). One by one the president's aides resigned. In an unrelated crime, Vice President Spiro Agnew admitted to filing a false tax return and also resigned. Investigators asked Nixon to give them copies of tapes that recorded his conversations in his offices. He finally released the tapes—with eighteen minutes erased from them. On the verge of being impeached for obstructing justice and violating his oath of office, in 1974 Nixon became the first and only American president to resign from office.

In all, fifty-six men were convicted of Watergate-related crimes. Some went to jail. Nixon was pardoned by his successor, Gerald Ford, a decision some people protested loudly. Others, President Ford included, thought it was best for the country to try to put the whole awful mess behind it.

AMERICAN VOICES

". . . THE PEOPLE HAVE GOT TO KNOW WHETHER OR NOT THEIR PRESIDENT IS A CROOK. WELL, I AM NOT A CROOK."

—PRESIDENT RICHARD NIXON, *1974*

What could women do in the early 1970s that they couldn't do before?

A couple of things. After 1972 they could take part in a much wider variety of high school and college sports. Title IX of the Educational Amendments passed by Congress that year said that public schools had to provide equal access and opportunities for women and girls in education if the schools received money from the government. These opportunities included sports, and they resulted in major change. Most schools had offered plenty of sports programs for boys but few, if any, for girls. In 1971 girls made up only 7.5 percent of U.S. high school athletes; by 1996 the figure was 39 percent.

In 1973 the Supreme Court gave women the ability to do something completely different with their bodies. The Court's ruling in the case of *Roe* v. *Wade* made abortions legal within the first three months of pregnancy. Before *Roe*, many women had abortions illegally and in unsafe conditions, which often caused complications, and sometimes even death. Poor women were especially at risk. The Court's decision in *Roe* v. *Wade* has been controversial ever since it was issued. Then as now, people who support the decision say the right to an abortion is a basic right to safety, privacy, and choice. Many opponents feel the decision amounts to government-approved murder.

What would you be sure to find at American gas stations in the mid–1970s?

Long lines and high prices. By the 1970s Americans had become very dependent on oil, not only for gas but also for heating homes and making products such as plastics and paint. America imported nearly half its oil supply, mostly from the oil-rich Arab countries of the Middle East. In 1973 the Arab nations attacked Israel in retaliation for land Israel had seized during a war in 1967. Because the United States was Israel's main ally, the Arab-controlled Organization of Petroleum Exporting Countries (OPEC) cut off oil shipments to the United States and reduced shipments to other countries.

For Americans and their oversized, gas-guzzling cars, the energy crisis was a huge wake-up call. The younger generations that hadn't experienced the sacrifices of the Great Depression and World War II suddenly knew what it was like to do without—and they didn't like it. As gas lines snaked around the block, violence broke out among frustrated drivers.

The Arab boycott was lifted in 1974, but the energy crisis made some people think about where they got their fuel, what kind of fuel they used, and how to conserve energy.

What was the "crisis of confidence"?

The energy crisis seemed to be just one thing that made Americans frustrated, skeptical, and disoriented in the 1970s. Vietnam and Watergate loomed large in people's memories, and as oil prices rose, so did unemployment and *inflation*. (Inflation means that prices rise and your money doesn't buy as much as it used to.) Combined, these things left many Americans feeling powerless and unsure of what they and their country were all about. President Carter said the country's lack of confidence threatened to destroy American democracy.

Jimmy Carter was a caring, approachable, and intelligent man. As president, he helped make an historic peace treaty between Egypt and Israel by inviting both countries' leaders to the presidential retreat at Camp David in 1978. But the Camp David Accord was overshadowed by a hostage crisis in Iran the following year, a crisis that confirmed many people's feeling that Carter wasn't a strong enough leader to handle the country's troubles.

The crisis started with a revolution in Iran. That country's ruler, the Shah, a longtime U.S. ally, was overthrown by the Ayatollah Khomeini. The Ayatollah hated the United States for supporting the Shah. In November 1979, five hundred Iranians loyal to Khomeini stormed the U.S. embassy in Tehran, Iran, and took fifty-two American diplomats hostage. The hostages were blindfolded and paraded in front of TV cameras while the Iranians yelled insults and burned the American flag. President Carter was determined to get the hostages home safely, but the rescue mission he ordered not only failed miserably, it left eight marines dead in the Iranian desert. It was an embarrassing disaster that made America look powerless and set the stage for more hostage-taking by Arabs. It also helped cost Carter the 1980 presidential election, which he lost by a landslide to Ronald Reagan. The Iranians got in one last jab at Carter by releasing the hostages just minutes after he left office.

What did President Reagan have in common with a frying pan?

Ronald Reagan has been called the "Teflon President" because there were many scandals during his administration, but none of them "stuck" to him. President Reagan was witty, old-fashioned, friendly, and optimistic. The oldest president to be elected, he turned seventy just after his inauguration. He'd made his living as a radio sportscaster, a TV host, and a Hollywood actor before going on to become governor of California. Reagan's background as an entertainer made him an inspiring speaker. People called him the "Great Communicator." His confidence and ease gave discouraged Americans a renewed patriotism and pride.

President Reagan's steady pressure on the Soviet Union is credited with helping to end the cold war. Still, Reagan's weakness was his dislike for details. He spoke in broad terms and handed many of his responsibilities to his staff. Some say he didn't pay much attention to what was going on around him. This inattention, combined with his affable nature, gave him the "Teflon" quality that let problems slide right off his back. During his administration, military interventions in Lebanon and the tiny Caribbean island of Granada cost American casualties; banking crises caused by lack of government watchfulness cost taxpayers billions of dollars; and the national debt quadrupled.

But one of the biggest scandals was the "Iran-Contra" Affair, which involved two sets of lies tangled into one big mess that stretched halfway around the globe. The affair involved the secret sale of missiles to Iran (one of America's enemies) in exchange for American hostages held by Iranian-supported Lebanese terrorists. Profits from the secret arms sale were used to send secret aid to a rebel army known as the "Contras" in Nicaragua. In 1984 Congress had cut off military aid to the Contras, who were fighting to overthrow the Communist-like Sandanistas in their country. The Iran-Contra scandal, which came to light in 1986, wasn't quite as bad as Watergate, but it was definitely illegal and unconstitutional. Two members of the National Security Council were later convicted of obstructing Congress. Reagan himself was never charged.

Why was the American space program put on hold in the 1980s?

Because of an awful disaster. The space shuttle *Challenger* had just taken off for its tenth flight in January 1986 when it exploded in the air, killing all seven people on board. Millions of people around the world were watching the lift-off because schoolteacher Christa McAuliffe was on board. McAuliffe, who'd been chosen to be the first teacher in space, was planning to broadcast lessons directly to schools from the shuttle's orbit around Earth.

The *Challenger* disaster led NASA to stop all space shuttle missions for nearly three years while the cause of the explosion, a faulty seal on one of the rocket boosters, was found and fixed. The teacher-in-space program was put on hold until the next century.

Why did Indiana teenager Ryan White have to fight for his right to go to school?

Because Ryan White had AIDS. AIDS (Acquired Immune Deficiency Syndrome) is a disease caused by infection with HIV (Human Immunodeficiency Virus), which attacks the body's immune system and its ability to resist other infections. AIDS is a *pandemic*, or a worldwide health crisis. But when the first cases were formally reported in 1981, no one knew what the mysterious disease was. AIDS was first detected in homosexual men, then in heterosexual men, in women, and in children. By the end of 2001, AIDS had killed 22 million people worldwide, including nearly a half million in the United States. An estimated 40 million more were living with HIV/AIDS.

Ryan White got HIV from a contaminated blood transfusion. He was diagnosed with AIDS in 1984, when he was thirteen. HIV can only be transmitted by a transfusion of blood or by having sex with an infected person, but many people then thought you could catch it from drinking fountains, toilet seats, shaking hands, sneezing, sweating, and sharing eating utensils. When word got out that Ryan had AIDS, his life changed dramatically. "Because of the lack of education on AIDS," he told the Presidential Commission on AIDS in 1988, "discrimination, fear, panic, and lies surrounded me. . . . I was labeled a troublemaker, and my mom an unfit mother, and I was not welcome anywhere. People would get up and leave, so they would not have to sit anywhere near me. Even at church, people would not shake my hand."

Ryan White fought nine months of court battles before he won the right to return to school. He continued to speak out about AIDS awareness and became known for his courage, determination, and pride. Ryan died in 1990, a year before he would have graduated from high school.

Could weathermen predict Desert Storm?

No, because it didn't have anything to do with the weather. Operation Desert Storm was the attack phase of the Persian Gulf War fought against Iraq in 1991. The Gulf War was fought against Iraq by a *coalition*, or a group of nations, led by the United States. It was a brief war in which America's military strength was overpowering. The attack against Iraq opened with fierce bombing and ended six weeks later with a hundred-hour ground war that drove Iraqi forces from Kuwait. The American-led coalition stopped short of invading Iraq and trying to overthrow its dictator, Saddam Hussein. But the great success with relatively few American losses made President George H. W. Bush very popular. For the first time since the terrible losses in Vietnam, many Americans felt confident about the American military once again. With the cooperation of so many other countries in the coalition, President Bush also felt hopeful that there would now be a "New World Order."

Part of his optimism about a world that worked more cooperatively came from another great change at that time. The long cold war between America and the Soviet Union was over. After decades of repressive rule, Communism had collapsed in many European countries in 1989 and 1990. The greatest symbol of the cold war, the Berlin Wall, which divided Communist East Berlin from democratic West Berlin, had been demolished in 1989. Communist East and democratic West Germany had been reunited. For a time it seemed that countries that were once enemies, including

★ Operation Desert Storm drove Saddam Hussein out of Kuwait, but the Gulf War ended with the Iraqi dictator still in power. After the war's end in 1991, Saddam continued to pose a problem to the world community. He was said to have used chemical weapons against his own people when they opposed him, and he kicked United Nations weapons inspectors out of his country—prompting many to wonder what he was hiding. Many people believe that dictatorial leaders such as Saddam Hussein are a threat to peace and stability in the Middle East and even the world.

the United States and Russia, could join together, as they did to defeat Saddam Hussein, and create a new era of international peace.

 "Debugging" a computer once meant removing the moths from inside it.

True! The first fully electronic computer, ENIAC, was built for use during World War II and shown to the public in 1946. ENIAC was no laptop—it took up an entire room and weighed thirty tons. The first computers were enormous, expensive, impractical, and complicated. They could break down if a small insect got inside them—hence the term *debugging*. But with the development of the microchip in 1971, several companies began building smaller computers that would fit on your desk at home or at work. In 1977 came the Apple computer, and in 1981 IBM introduced the personal computer (PC). Computers have been getting smaller and more powerful ever since.

Computers and microchips are the backbone of the technology revolution that continues to change peoples' lives and

economy today. Now we have cellular phones, digital cameras, Palm Pilots, MP-3 players, and all sorts of other gadgets that are made possible by the microchip. But possibly the most significant development of the "information age" is the Internet. Like the first computers, the Internet was developed by the U.S. military and researchers at universities. It entered mainstream America in the early 1990s, and soon, millions were "surfing" the Internet via the World Wide Web. The Internet has changed the way we live, think, shop, learn, and communicate. People across the country or around the globe can meet and connect online; the world seems smaller now.

AMERICAN ★ STORIES

What famous billionaire dropped out of college?

Bill Gates, chairman of Microsoft Corporation. Bill Gates began programming computers when he was just thirteen. That was back in 1968, when computers were the size of refrigerators. But Bill Gates believed that one day smaller computers would be on every desk in every home and office. Those computers would need software to run them. Six years later Bill Gates dropped out of college at Harvard to found Microsoft Corporation with a childhood friend. Soon you almost couldn't run a personal computer if you didn't have Microsoft software (MS-DOS, then Windows). In 2000 *Forbes* magazine listed Gates as the richest man in the world for the sixth year in a row. He and his wife, Melinda, have given away billions of dollars for global health care, American libraries and education, community programs near their home in the Pacific Northwest, and other special projects.

What did President Bill Clinton have in common with President Andrew Johnson?

He was impeached. President Clinton was charismatic, hardworking, and uncommonly smart. The boy from small-town Arkansas could read before he was three and is the only president to have been a Rhodes scholar at Oxford University in England. As president, Clinton balanced the budget and presided over a roaring economy with low unemployment. He established freer trade with Canada and Mexico with the North American Free Trade Agreement (NAFTA) in 1993 and signed the Brady Bill for handgun control.

Clinton ran into trouble when the public found out he was having a relationship with a young White House intern named Monica Lewinsky. When questioned, Clinton denied the relationship, lying to the nation and to members of his administration. For these lies, Clinton was impeached by the House of Representatives in 1998. But like Johnson, the Senate did not find him guilty of the "high crimes and misdemeanors" needed to remove a president from office.

Clinton did things that most people considered immoral. He also lied in a court case, which is usually considered a crime.

But those things were finally not considered serious enough offenses by the Senate, though he did lose some privileges as a lawyer, his profession before he entered politics. How will history judge President Clinton? Will he be remembered as the leader of America during a time of peace and prosperity? Or as the second president to be impeached? It is hard to say so soon after he left office.

Were the 1990s an age of rage?

In many ways, yes. More and more, violence became an outlet for the frustration, disagreement, and discontent of people who felt left behind in the fast-moving America of the nineties. A month after President Clinton took office, an *Islamic fundamentalist* (someone who believes in rigidly following an extreme version of the Muslim religion) bombed the World Trade Center in New York, killing six and wounding more than a thousand. Two months later, an FBI raid on the Branch Davidian religious compound in Waco, Texas, left more than eighty of the cult members dead. Two years later, in response, antigovernment extremists Timothy McVeigh and Terry Nichols exploded a bomb outside the Murrah Federal Building in Oklahoma City. The explosion killed 169 people, including 19 children who were at the building's day-care center.

There was race-related violence, too. In 1991 four white Los Angeles police officers pulled over a black driver named Rodney King for speeding. They dragged King from his car and kicked and beat him with nightsticks. The incident was caught on home video and shown on the news, enraging Americans across the country. Yet the policemen were acquitted in 1992. A riot broke out in Los Angeles. Over two days protesters set hundreds of fires and looted millions of dollars' worth of merchandise from stores. Fifty-four people died.

There was even violence in schools. In the late 1990s thousands of students were expelled for bringing guns or other firearms to public schools. Some students who were not caught went on rampages, killing and wounding students and teachers. The worst of these occurred at Columbine High

School in Littleton, Colorado, in 1999. Two boys killed twelve students and a teacher before shooting themselves. Some people blamed school violence on the media—violent video games, movies, television shows, and music—and others blamed parents who were out of touch with their children.

Why was George W. Bush declared president twice—in the same election?

Because the race between Bush (the son of former president George H. W. Bush) and his opponent, Al Gore, was so close that it was difficult to tell who won the electoral vote. (Gore won the popular vote, but it's the electoral vote that counts.) For much of the campaign, Bush and Gore had been neck and neck, and they stayed that way even after the election.

On election night television stations counting the election returns estimated that Gore had won the key state of Florida. As more results came in from that state, however, the stations retracted the estimate, saying Florida was still undecided. Meanwhile, results from other states came in and made it clear that the race hinged on which candidate won the most votes in Florida. In the early hours of the morning, the networks said it was Bush who had won the state where Bush's brother Jeb was governor. But then they took *that* back, saying Florida, and thus the race in general, was "too close to call."

In the first count of the Florida votes, Bush was ahead by eighteen hundred, but Florida law says that if the margin is less than two thousand votes, the ballots must be recounted. For thirty-six days, Americans—including the candidates— waited in suspense while votes were counted again and again. Finally, in a controversial decision, the U.S. Supreme Court overturned the Florida Supreme Court's ruling allowing the ballots to be counted by hand. That meant Bush's narrow lead in Florida would stand. Bush would be the next president.

When George W. Bush was inaugurated on January 20, 2001, he became the second American president to be the son of a former president. (Do you know who was the first father-son pair? Hint: The father was the second president, his son the sixth.) But many Americans believed he had really lost to Al Gore. Though the contest had been bitter and sometimes ugly, Gore gave a gracious concession speech in which he called on Americans to unite behind the new president.

★ The election of 2000 marked the fourth time in U.S. history, and the first time in more than a hundred years, that the president hadn't won the popular vote. The close election made people ask whether states should update old-fashioned voting equipment and reform or get rid of the electoral college (which would require a constitutional amendment). Because the election had been so tight, it left some Americans feeling that every vote counts. But because some votes had been tossed out for being unreadable, others felt just the opposite.

What happened on September 11, 2001, that shocked the world?

The worst terrorist attack ever on U.S. soil. On a perfect, sunny, late-summer morning, four American airplanes were *hijacked*, or taken over, by terrorists. The terrorists flew two planes into the two 110-story World Trade Center towers in New York City and another plane into the Pentagon (our military headquarters) in Washington, D.C. The fourth plane crashed in an empty field southeast of Pittsburgh, Pennsylvania, on its

way to Washington. Almost three
thousand people were killed in the
attack. More Americans died then
than in the Japanese attack on Pearl
Harbor during World War II.
Among the dead
were more than three
hundred heroic New
York City firefighters and
police officers who were in the
Trade Center towers to rescue others
when the buildings collapsed.

The September 11 "Attack on America" left people scared,
shocked, and filled with grief. Until September 11 Americans
had viewed terrorism as something that happened in other
countries, not at home. The United States is the richest and
most powerful country in the world; its citizens thought they
were invincible. In less than two hours, they learned that they
were not. Yet the attack, designed to bring Americans down, in
many ways made them stronger—a sort of re-United States. It
made people think about what it means to be an American. It
showed them real-life heroes in the firefighters, police officers,
medical personnel, and rescue workers who rushed to the
sites, and in the millions of others who gave food, clothing,
services, or money to help the victims and their families.

AMERICAN VOICES

"GREAT HARM HAS BEEN DONE TO US. WE HAVE SUFFERED GREAT
LOSS. AND IN OUR GRIEF AND ANGER WE HAVE FOUND OUR
MISSION AND OUR MOMENT.

"FREEDOM AND FEAR ARE AT WAR. THE ADVANCE OF HUMAN
FREEDOM, THE GREAT ACHIEVEMENT OF OUR TIME AND THE GREAT
HOPE OF EVERY TIME, NOW DEPENDS ON US.

> "OUR NATION, THIS GENERATION, WILL LIFT THE DARK THREAT OF VIOLENCE FROM OUR PEOPLE AND OUR FUTURE. WE WILL RALLY THE WORLD TO THIS CAUSE BY OUR EFFORTS, BY OUR COURAGE. WE WILL NOT TIRE, WE WILL NOT FALTER AND WE WILL NOT FAIL."
>
> —*President* GEORGE W. BUSH, *addressing Congress and the nation,*
> *September 20, 2001*

Who hijacked the planes on September 11, and why?

Almost immediately after the September 11 attacks, President Bush declared a war on terrorism and rallied dozens of nations to America's side. Few took much persuading, as some eighty countries had also lost citizens who were visiting or working in the United States. But this war is not against any country, or even a visible enemy. (Some people say it shouldn't be called a "war" at all, since wars are fought between nations.) Terrorist groups often spin tangled webs all across the globe. So this is a war of intelligence, diplomacy, and prevention even more than one of military might.

The attacks came from a small number of Islamic fundamentalists. The terrorists were led by a wealthy Saudi Arabian man named Osama bin Laden. In general, terrorists aim to spread fear that keeps people and institutions from working and thereby deny them the freedom that keeps the country alive. These terrorists specifically have a special hatred for America because they disagree with American culture and values (such as freedom, diversity, modernity, pursuit of self-interest, and separation of church and state). They are also angry about actions America has taken in the Arab world since the Persian Gulf War, and about the country's support of Israel in its conflicts with Arab Palestinians over both the creation of a Palestinian homeland and shared holy sites in Jerusalem. These are not issues that will be quickly or easily resolved.

By 2050, the U.S. Census Bureau projects that only 53 percent of Americans will be

a) black

c) green

b) non-Hispanic white

d) eating their vegetables

The answer is letter *b*. We have always been a nation of immigrants, but that's never been more true than it is today. Since the government got rid of immigration quotas based on nationality in 1965, the United States has seen a major wave of newcomers. When the United States left Vietnam in 1975, hundreds of thousands of refugees from Southeast Asia fled their countries, many in small boats, hoping to arrive in America safely. Immigrants have also come from China, Cuba, the Philippines, Mexico, and other parts of Latin America. Twenty-seven million immigrants have arrived since 1965, and the Census Bureau estimates that 80 million more will reach the United States by 2050. At that point, the American population is expected to be 53 percent white (non-Hispanic), 25 percent Hispanic, 14 percent black, 8 percent Asian and Pacific, and 1 percent Indian, Eskimo, and Aleut. That will make people of Spanish-speaking origin the largest ethnic group in the United States.

About one-fourth of immigrants enter illegally, many crossing the two-thousand-mile border with Mexico. Others come legally, to be reunited with family members, to work, or to seek refuge from life in war-torn nations. Some Americans say that high levels of immigration put jobs and the environment at risk, but many believe it promotes diversity and increases the number of creative minds and with it, the pace of innovation. As the nation becomes more diverse, one thing most people can agree on: With its unique medley of colors, religions, talents, and opportunities, the United States is still a symbol of freedom and hope for the world.

Presidents and Their Vice Presidents

OFFICE	NAME	YEARS
PRESIDENT	**George Washington**	**1789–1797**
VICE PRESIDENT	John Adams	1789–1797
PRESIDENT	**John Adams**	**1797–1801**
VICE PRESIDENT	Thomas Jefferson	1797–1801
PRESIDENT	**Thomas Jefferson**	**1801–1809**
VICE PRESIDENT	Aaron Burr	1801–1805
VICE PRESIDENT	George Clinton	1805–1809
PRESIDENT	**James Madison**	**1809–1817**
VICE PRESIDENT	George Clinton	1809–1812
VICE PRESIDENT	Elbridge Gerry	1812–1814
PRESIDENT	**James Monroe**	**1817–1825**
VICE PRESIDENT	Daniel D. Tompkins	1817–1825
PRESIDENT	**John Quincy Adams**	**1825–1829**
VICE PRESIDENT	John C. Calhoun	1825–1829
PRESIDENT	**Andrew Jackson**	**1829–1837**
VICE PRESIDENT	John C. Calhoun	1829–1832
VICE PRESIDENT	Martin Van Buren	1833–1837
PRESIDENT	**Martin Van Buren**	**1837–1841**
VICE PRESIDENT	Richard M. Johnson	1837–1841
PRESIDENT	**William Henry Harrison**	**1841**
VICE PRESIDENT	John Tyler	1841
PRESIDENT	**John Tyler**	**1841–1845**
PRESIDENT	**James K. Polk**	**1845–1849**
VICE PRESIDENT	George M. Dallas	1845–1849
PRESIDENT	**Zachary Taylor**	**1849–1850**
VICE PRESIDENT	Millard Fillmore	1849–1850

| PRESIDENT | Millard Fillmore | 1850–1853 |

PRESIDENT	Franklin Pierce	1853–1857
VICE PRESIDENT	William R. King	1853

PRESIDENT	James Buchanan	1857–1861
VICE PRESIDENT	John C. Breckinridge	1857–1861

PRESIDENT	Abraham Lincoln	1861–1865
VICE PRESIDENT	Hannibal Hamlin	1861–1865
VICE PRESIDENT	Andrew Johnson	1865

PRESIDENT	Andrew Johnson	1865–1869

PRESIDENT	Ulysses S. Grant	1869–1877
VICE PRESIDENT	Schuyler Colfax	1869–1873
VICE PRESIDENT	Henry Wilson	1873–1875

PRESIDENT	Rutherford B. Hayes	1877–1881
VICE PRESIDENT	William A. Wheeler	1877–1881

PRESIDENT	James A. Garfield	1881
VICE PRESIDENT	Chester A. Arthur	1881

PRESIDENT	Chester A. Arthur	1881–1885

PRESIDENT	Grover Cleveland	1885–1889
VICE PRESIDENT	Thomas A. Hendricks	1885

PRESIDENT	Benjamin Harrison	1889–1893
VICE PRESIDENT	Levi P. Morton	1889–1893

PRESIDENT	Grover Cleveland	1893–1897
VICE PRESIDENT	Adlai E. Stevenson	1893–1897

PRESIDENT	William McKinley	1897–1901
VICE PRESIDENT	Garret A. Hobart	1897–1899
VICE PRESIDENT	Theodore Roosevelt	1901

PRESIDENT	Theodore Roosevelt	1901–1909
VICE PRESIDENT	Charles W. Fairbanks	1905–1909

PRESIDENT	William H. Taft	1909–1913
VICE PRESIDENT	James S. Sherman	1909–1912

PRESIDENT	Woodrow Wilson	1913–1921
VICE PRESIDENT	Thomas R. Marshall	1913–1921

PRESIDENT	**Warren G. Harding**	**1921–1923**
VICE PRESIDENT	Calvin Coolidge	1921–1923
PRESIDENT	**Calvin Coolidge**	**1923–1929**
VICE PRESIDENT	Charles G. Dawes	1925–1929
PRESIDENT	**Herbert Hoover**	**1929–1933**
VICE PRESIDENT	Charles Curtis	1929–1933
PRESIDENT	**Franklin D. Roosevelt**	**1933–1945**
VICE PRESIDENT	John N. Garner	1933–1941
VICE PRESIDENT	Henry A. Wallace	1941–1945
VICE PRESIDENT	Harry S. Truman	1945
PRESIDENT	**Harry S. Truman**	**1945–1953**
VICE PRESIDENT	Alben W. Barkley	1949–1953
PRESIDENT	**Dwight D. Eisenhower**	**1953–1961**
VICE PRESIDENT	Richard M. Nixon	1953–1961
PRESIDENT	**John F. Kennedy**	**1961–1963**
VICE PRESIDENT	Lyndon B. Johnson	1961–1963
PRESIDENT	**Lyndon B. Johnson**	**1963–1969**
VICE PRESIDENT	Hubert H. Humphrey	1965–1969
PRESIDENT	**Richard M. Nixon**	**1969–1974**
VICE PRESIDENT	Spiro Agnew	1969–1973
VICE PRESIDENT	Gerald R. Ford	1973–1974
PRESIDENT	**Gerald R. Ford**	**1974–1977**
VICE PRESIDENT	Nelson A. Rockefeller	1974–1977
PRESIDENT	**James Earl (Jimmy) Carter**	**1977–1981**
VICE PRESIDENT	Walter F. Mondale	1977–1981
PRESIDENT	**Ronald Reagan**	**1981–1989**
VICE PRESIDENT	George H. W. Bush	1981–1989
PRESIDENT	**George H. W. Bush**	**1989–1993**
VICE PRESIDENT	J. Danforth Quayle	1989–1993
PRESIDENT	**William J. (Bill) Clinton**	**1993–2001**
VICE PRESIDENT	Albert Gore, Jr.	1993–2001
PRESIDENT	**George W. Bush**	**2001–**
VICE PRESIDENT	Richard M. Cheney	2001–

Ambrose, Stephen E. *Citizen Soldiers*. New York: Simon & Schuster, 1997.

———. *Nothing Like It in the World: The Men Who Built the Transcontinental Railroad 1863–1869*. New York: Simon & Schuster, 2000.

———. *Undaunted Courage: Meriwether Lewis, Thomas Jefferson, and the Opening of the American West*. New York: Simon & Schuster, 1996.

Ambrose, Stephen E., and Douglas Brinkley, eds. *Witness to America*. New York: HarperCollins Publishers, 1999.

Axelrod, Alan, and Charles Phillips. *What Every American Should Know About American History*. Holbrook, Mass.: Adams Media Corporation, 1992.

Blumberg, Rhoda. *What's the Deal?: Jefferson, Napoleon, and the Louisiana Purchase*. Washington, D.C.: National Geographic Society, 1998.

Boller, Paul F., Jr. *Not So! Popular Myths About America from Columbus to Clinton*. New York: Oxford University Press, 1995.

Brokaw, Tom. *The Greatest Generation*. New York: Random House, 1998.

Bryson, Bill. *Made in America*. New York: Avon Books, 1994.

Ciment, James. *The Young People's History of the United States*. New York: Barnes & Noble Books, 1998.

Colbert, David. *Eyewitness to America*. New York: Pantheon Books, 1997.

Davidson, James West, and Mark Hamilton Lytle. *After the Fact: The Art of Historical Detection*. Vol. II. New York: McGraw-Hill, 1992.

Davis, Kenneth C. *Don't Know Much About® History*. New York: Avon Books, 1990.

DeGregario, William A. *The Complete Book of U.S. Presidents*. New York: Barricade Books, 1993.

Douglass, Frederick. *Narrative of the Life of Frederick Douglass, an American Slave*. New York: Penguin, 1992.

Ellis, Joseph. *American Sphinx: The Character of Thomas Jefferson*. New York: Vintage Books, 1996.

———. *Founding Brothers: The Revolutionary Generation*. New York: Alfred A. Knopf, 2000.

Ferling, John. *Setting the World Ablaze: Washington, Adams, Jefferson, and the American Revolution*. New York: Oxford University Press, 2000.

Fleming, Thomas. *Liberty! The American Revolution*. New York: Viking Penguin, 1997.

Flexner, Stuart Berg. *I Hear America Talking*. New York: Touchstone Books, 1976.

Flexner, Stuart Berg, and Anne H. Soukhanov. *Speaking Freely: A Guided Tour of American English*. New York: Oxford University Press, 1997.

Goodwin, Doris Kearns. *No Ordinary Time: Franklin and Eleanor Roosevelt: The Home Front in World War II*. New York: Touchstone Books, 1995.

Hakim, Joy. *The History of US*. 11 volumes. New York: Oxford University Press, 1999.

Halberstam, David. *The Fifties*. New York: Fawcett Books, 1994.

Hawke, David Freeman. *Everyday Life in Early America*. New York: Harper & Row Publishers, 1988.

Hazen, Walter A. *Everyday Life: The Civil War*. Parsippany, N.J.: Good Year Books, 1999.

———. *Everyday Life: Revolutionary War*. Parsippany, N.J.: Good Year Books, 2000.

Heinemann, Sue. *The New York Public Library Amazing Women in American History*. New York: John Wiley & Sons, 1998.

Hoose, Phillip. *We Were There, Too!: Young People in U.S. History*. New York: Farrar, Straus & Giroux, 2001.

Jennings, Peter, and Todd Brewster. *The Century for Young People*. New York: Doubleday Books for Young Readers, 1999.

Keenan, Sheila. *Scholastic Encyclopedia of Women in the United States*. New York: Scholastic, 1996.

Kerber, Linda K., and Jane Sherron DeHart. *Women's America*. New York: Oxford University Press, 1991.

Marin, Albert. *Sitting Bull and His World*. New York: Dutton Books, 2000.

McCullough, David. *John Adams*. New York: Simon & Schuster, 2001.

Patrick, Diane. *The New York Public Library Amazing African American History*. New York: John Wiley & Sons, 1998.

Reader's Digest Strange Stories, Amazing Facts of America's Past. Pleasantville, N.Y.: The Reader's Digest Association, 1989.

Rubel, David. *Scholastic Encyclopedia of the Presidents and Their Times*. New York: Scholastic, 1994.

Schlereth, Thomas J. *Victorian America*. New York: HarperCollins Publishers, 1991.

Shenkman, Richard. *Legends, Lies, & Cherished Myths of American History*. New York: William Morrow, 1988.

Sinclair, Andrew. *A Concise History of the United States*. Phoenix Mill, England: Sutton Publishing, 1999.

Stevenson, Jay, and Matthew Budman. *The Complete Idiot's Guide to American Heroes*. New York: Alpha Books, 1999.

Stolley, Richard. *Life: Our Century in Pictures for Young People*. Boston: Little, Brown, 2000.

Unruh, John D., Jr. *The Plains Across*. Urbana: University of Illinois Press, 1979.

Ward, Geoffrey C. *The West*. Boston: Little, Brown, 1996.

Winik, Jay. *April 1865: The Month That Saved America*. New York: HarperCollins Publishers, 2001.

Zinn, Howard. *A People's History of the United States 1492–Present*. New York: HarperCollins Publishers, 1999.

973
DAV

Davis, Kenneth C.

American history

DATE DUE			
OCT 2 3 2008			
SEP 2 2 2008			
OCT 0 6 2008			